THE 7 HEAVENLY VIRTUES
OF LEADERSHIP

THE 7 HEAVENLY VIRTUES
OF LEADERSHIP

MANAGEMENT
TODAY SERIES

AUSTRALIAN
INSTITUTE OF
MANAGEMENT

Series Editors
Carolyn Barker
and
Robyn Coy

Sydney New York San Francisco Auckland Bogotá Caracas
Lisbon London Madrid MexicoCity Milan Montreal New Delhi
SanJuan Singapore Tokyo Toronto

Copying for educational purposes

National Library of Australia Cataloguing-in-Publication data:

The 7 heavenly virtues of leadership.

Bibliography.
Includes index.
ISBN 0 074 71258 6.

1. Leadership. 2. Management – Australia. I. Barker,
Carolyn. (Series: Management today (McGraw-Hill)).

658.400994

Published in Australia by
McGraw-Hill Australia Pty Ltd
Level 2, 82 Waterloo Road, North Ryde NSW 2113
Acquisitions Editor: Javier Dopico
Production Editor: Sybil Kesteven
Editor: Sharon Nevile
Proofreader: Tim Learner
Indexer: Linda Cross
Designer (cover and interior): Lucy Bal
Cover image: gettyimages
Illustrator: Alan Laver, Shelly Communications
Typeset in Bembo by Post Pre-press Group
Printed on 80 gsm woodfree by Pantech Limited, Hong Kong.

The **McGraw·Hill** *Companies*

CONTENTS

PREFACE

Whenever we act with virtue, show good character or demonstrate moral or ethical behaviour, it is an act of will. Virtue is not innate, it is something that is developed and enacted through choice. Furthermore, it can be developed over time. Like all acts of will, it can be reinforced by reward and punishment. As Aristotle said: 'We become virtuous by practising virtue'. Growing in this way is all about discovery, enactment, role modelling and, most importantly, ownership.

This is the backdrop we have chosen for this book, which is an investigation of the impact on the organisation of virtuous behaviour by an individual. It is our contention that that healthy, positive and aligned organisations are shaped by leaders who are seen by their followers as being virtuous. And given the current worldwide focus on management actions that have led to corporate collapse, organisational transparency, and the role of ethical behaviour, what better time to consider the integration of leadership and virtue?

The 7 Heavenly Virtues of Leadership comprises a series of specially commissioned chapters that define the personal dimensions of leadership. It is an exploration of the domain where the 'leadership buck' stops—where there is no-one to answer to but self.

Underpinning leadership with virtue is the concept of the 'ripple effect'. Virtue at the top ripples through the organisation, affecting the staff, the stakeholders, shareholders, suppliers and customers, and also corporate citizenship. In the corporate context, it is about using good behaviour to drive the bottom line.

We asked our chapter authors to expand the boundaries of the leadership discussion beyond organisational, management and business dimensions to reveal personal, social and spiritual dimensions. We included the word 'heavenly' in the title, to denote the potential progression of the leadership journey into a symbolic higher realm. The use of the word 'virtue' signals that there is a moral anchor to leadership, which is bound up with self-knowledge and what an individual values—a notion uncomfortable for some, but liberating for others.

In quantifying the leadership virtues, it became apparent that, although we are all familiar with the seven deadly sins (a concept so embedded in our social psyche that we see it in everything from movies to ice creams and lipsticks), a list of leadership virtues relevant for modern Australian organisations was not generally defined. Our subsequent research and discussions with practising managers and leaders from around the country resulted in a final list of seven leadership virtues: *humility, courage, integrity, compassion, humour, passion* and *wisdom*. It should be noted that, although six of these virtues seemed obvious choices, there was considerable debate over the inclusion of humour. In the end it became clear that humour is very much a part of today's psyche, especially in Australian organisations.

Interestingly, at the same time that we embarked on this project, an international group of researchers began a study of a huge range of cultures, from ancient times to modern, to discover whether there were any universal concepts of good character (or virtues). They discovered that there were no *universal* virtues, but that there were six that were *ubiquitous* (that is, endorsed by almost all religious and philosophical traditions). These were further divided into 24 'character strengths' (see Martin Seligman's *Authentic Happiness*, 2002). We were pleased to discover that our selection of virtues paralleled this framework.

At the core of this book is the almost old-fashioned notion of *character*—more specifically, *good character* . . . what Abraham Lincoln called 'the better angels of our nature'. During the Darwinian struggle for corporate survival over the past two decades, Lincoln's 'better angels' seemed forgotten and out of fashion. However, they and the concept of virtuous leadership are again emerging as a realistic and viable framework for organisations and individuals.

Some would argue that character traits are not the same as behaviour, and that it is behaviour that determines leadership capability. It is the translation process of character and virtue into behaviour and action that is the focus of this book.

Do not mistake this approach to leadership as 'soft'. This is hard stuff. It means recognising that management and leadership involves more than models and theory (though they have their place). It's about discovering what really matters to *you;* being brave enough to acknowledge it; and then finding a way to live, work and lead that is congruent.

Our list of virtues is not a prescription for the 'right-thinking' leader. It is not our contention that leaders are saintly. The motivation to act with virtue can be altruistic or anchored in self-interest. Indeed, the current rush for corporate transparency and stronger governance may have more to do with avoiding exposure for wrongdoing (and the associated shareholder backlash) than with a commitment to truth, justice and ethics. Does this matter? We think not. To quote a wise saying: 'You can do no harm by acting virtuously'.

It is proper to note that our chapter authors do not hold themselves to be paragons of the virtues they describe. Rather, they were selected because of their willingness to speak from the heart about their experiences of leadership and leading. We asked them to combine intellectual rigour with personal and passionate opinion, and to expose their hopes and longings for the future of leadership. We honour them for their courage and wisdom (virtuous behaviour, indeed).

In picking up this book, it is likely that you are already predisposed to the concept of virtuous leadership. The book's structure allows you to choose the virtue that you connect with the most, dip into each self-contained chapter and then immerse yourself in its content and follow the direction the author has taken. You will find that each virtue overlaps with one or more of the others, prompting you to investigate other chapters according to your needs.

The *Management Today Series*

It would seem that we are fundamentally changing the way we work and manage, but what does that mean for those who would call themselves 'leader'? The *Management Today Series* is AIM's response to that question.

The first book in the series, *Innovation and Imagination at Work*, canvassed the topic of innovation and creativity from a range of perspectives—from entrepreneurial endeavour to right-brained creativity and 'future thinking'. However, the underlying theme of all chapters was *leadership* and the impact (for better or worse) of the individual leader on the innovation process.

In *The Heart and Soul of Leadership*, the second book in the series, our authors pulled apart what it means to be a leader in an organisational setting in Australia. Macro issues and organisational models were juxtaposed with a full-frontal exposure of the emotional aspects of leading.

For our third book, *The Uncertain Art of Management*, we commissioned author Harry Onsman to provide a guide through the maze that is everyday management. This practical, commonsense book was underpinned by the compassionate notion that, as a manager, you can't (in fact, won't) get it right every time. There is no one 'best' way to manage . . . but there is always a better way if you are willing to look for it. Much of the book explores leadership—how could it not when one of the enduring definitions of management is 'to plan, implement, control, evaluate and *lead*'.

In this, the fourth book, our editorial journey parallels the wider, ongoing quest to understand and resolve the ambiguities of leadership . . . the personal quest that we believe many of you have already commenced.

If you have a response or comment, or wish to challenge any of the propositions found in the book, please email us at editor@aim.com.au or visit www.aim.com.au. As always, we look forward to your feedback.

Carolyn Barker, FAIM and **Robyn Coy, AIMM**
Series Editors
Australian Institute of Management

HUMILITY 1

Mark Strom

ABOUT THE AUTHOR

Mark Strom, PhD, FAICD

Mark Strom has partnered people in many walks of life as they transform their organisations and communities. His clients have included mining companies, financial institutions, federal and state government agencies, and not for profit organisations.

He is an inter-disciplinary thinker, a philosopher interested in asking the questions that help build 'partnerships in living well', and an historian of ideas with a bent for reading social systems. The heart of his work is to deconstruct bureaucratic artifice and the mythologies of culture and change, to identify crucial missing conversations and bring them to life, to mentor design thinking, and to teach that wisdom is the heart of leadership.

Mark first read theology, then philosophy and ancient history. His doctoral research was an interdisciplinary study of the intellectual and social contexts and conventions of leadership in the first century and the present. The work has been acclaimed for its scholarly and practical implications.

Mark is a Fellow of the Australian Institute of Company Directors and is the author of *Reframing Paul: Conversations in Grace and Community* (InterVarsity Press).

Mark Strom can be reached at mstrom@hawknet.com.au.

Introduction

A new chief executive faces the debris of mismanagement and cronyism—poor financials, poor operations, poor quality, poor safety, dispirited people and a lacklustre executive team. Many will have to work harder before they work smarter. Some may have to go. She feels she could do their work better in half the time. What is needed? A little arrogance to shake the place up? A little humility to soften the cynicism? She can't afford this introspection. There are changes to be made.

Why does she struggle? The experts say there is no tension between people and performance. The cliches tell her that people are her 'greatest resource', 'highest priority' and the 'key to performance'. Yet the sheer pressure to perform makes it so easy to shelve 'people matters'. More tellingly, she refuses to label people as 'resources', 'keys' or 'priorities'. She senses the incongruence between a view of the world as measurable and manageable, with people as things to be managed, and a view of the world that ties leadership to character. Should they obey her because of her rank? Or should she earn their respect by her character? There *is* a tension and it has a long history.

This new CEO faces a tangle of ideas and ideals around virtue and leadership that has persisted throughout the history of Western ideas and society. Humility is part of that tangle. We need to appreciate this history to better understand our own challenges.

On virtue and leadership

There is a long tradition of defining leadership by virtues. It was the standard approach of philosophers and orators, widely attested in literature, inscriptions and personal correspondence from classical times, through the Roman Empire and Middle Ages, and down to the present. Today, benefactors and heroes are praised for their virtues on monuments and plaques in our own cities. But the ancients would not approve our list of virtues. They would think us queer, confused and liable to undermine the good order of society. And they would never call humility a virtue for leaders.

The classical tradition

In the ancient worlds of Greece and Rome, leadership meant rank—position, not role. Leadership was a right and responsibility attached to a man (overwhelmingly a man) by birth, marriage or adoption. Leadership did not depend on competence, gift, intellect or experience. Its purpose was to maintain the order of a highly stratified society. Good order depended on people staying in the places allotted to them by birth, by fate, by the gods or by personal accomplishment.

Looking back, it might seem that leadership positions were filled as a matter of course by some benign social process, but this was not the case. We need to appreciate the difference between rank and status. Rank was largely fixed by birth, with some chance at change through marriage or adoption (hence we read of great men with sons many years their senior). Status was another matter. Its marks are familiar to us: education, wealth, fame, achievements, friendships, personal appearance, memberships, lifestyle. So, a man might live many steps above or below his rank according to how well he fared in business and in securing the right friends.

Imagine a social network akin to a modern pyramid scheme. This was how the classical world worked—a vast web of patron–client relationships carrying formal obligations and conventions. People worked to have others obligated to themselves, and called upon the conventions of enmity when slighted. This was the social reality behind the sermonising on friendship by the likes of Plato or Seneca. Those within most layers of the pyramid never worked a day in their lives. Work with the hands was unseemly, and this included what we would call administration or management. Those above took a share of what was achieved below.

Strange as it may seem to us, money flowed *down* as well as up the pyramid. What did patrons stand to gain? Support. Prestige. Influence. The harmony and wellbeing of the *polis* (the city or state) depended on public works, the dole (in times of famine), religious observances, festivals and games. Relatively few of these were financed by public monies. The money came from benefactors—the men at the top and those keen to impress. Friendship meant reciprocity. There were no free lunches in Athens or Rome. Layer upon layer of freeborn men, and not a few entrepreneurial freedmen, spent the bulk of their days in lobbying and intrigue, subterfuge and toadying. Litigation was rampant.

This is our context for understanding virtue in times past. Virtue was tied to ambition, both of the individual and of the *polis*. Indeed, the love of ambition was itself considered a virtue. Men and women competed to be known as virtuous. Virtue was a point of comparison, a competitive advantage. The social conventions of leadership were to maintain rank and to allow the trading of status. With this social context in mind, we can better consider the individual virtues as the marks of noble leaders.

Four virtues were supreme in philosophical and popular thought—courage (manliness), justice, self-control (temperance) and wisdom. This book includes only two of these ancient virtues: courage and wisdom. The ancients would *never* have included the rest of our topics: compassion, humility, humour, passion or integrity. Compassion was a weakness. Humility may possibly have been a virtue for a woman, but never for a man. Humour was unseemly (notwithstanding the many great one-liners and gags of the satirists). Passion disturbed the fine balance of the noble man. Integrity, too, was tied to social convention—people were expected to act not in accordance with their private values (a concept foreign to Greeks and Romans alike), but in keeping with what was expected of their social standing.

Love of ambition was a virtue. Wisdom was the mark of the man who read the political moods and timed well his move up the ladder.

Like leadership, indeed *because* of leadership, virtue was tied to rank. Only the elite were capable of virtue. Only the elite knew best. If a noble man judged that lying to the masses was in the best interests of the *polis*, then to lie *was* virtuous. Even the two virtues we share with the ancients—courage and wisdom—were thoroughly cast in the service of rank and power. Courage equated to manliness—hence the censure on gentleness or compassion.

We still quote the Delphic maxim: 'Know yourself'. We might better translate it: 'Know your *place*'. Of the more than 250 such moral maxims in wide circulation over almost a millennium, the fab four were these: 'Know yourself'; 'Nothing to excess'; 'A price for commitments'; and 'Pick your time'. We can hear the tones of rank and status. Compassion and humility hinder ambition . . . keep compassion for those who deserve it . . . don't exceed what is socially expected, or there'll be a price to pay . . . so stay in your place while you wait your chance.

Mercy, love or grace never figured as virtues. Neither did humility. They were blemishes, excesses and liabilities. The gods agreed. Humility was no more a 'heavenly' virtue than an earthly one. The affairs of men mirrored the soap operas of the gods. There was nothing divine about humility. Not, at least, in the Greek and Roman traditions.

The classical virtues—courage, justice, self-control and wisdom—were structured and controlled by rank and status. There are similar lists in Oriental traditions. Confucius is credited with saying: 'Wisdom, benevolence and courage, these three are virtues universally acknowledged in the Empire.' Benevolence is the mark of the gentleman. The idea and social context are coloured by the demands of rank and status, not unlike the world of the Greeks and Romans. As Aristotle said, 'If the gentleman forsakes benevolence, in what way can he make a name for himself?' The good order of society required balance, order, the middle path between extremes. 'Virtue . . . observes the mean relative to us . . . We call it a mean condition as lying between two forms of badness, one being excess and the other deficiency.' Confucius makes a similar point: 'Supreme indeed is the Mean as a moral virtue. It has been rare among the common people for quite a long time.'

Good order required benefactors. Given the dependence of both individuals and the *polis* upon benefactions, it was in everyone's interests to support the big man. Thus the inscriptions. They were propaganda. They told the sons of the big man and his peers what they must live up to. They told lesser mortals that they were inferior, and rightly so. The virtuous leader was an ideal and a social necessity. For Seneca, the Roman senator and philosopher, the virtuous leader aimed at self-protection. There was little place for humility:

Know, therefore, Serenus, that this perfect man, full of virtues human and divine, can lose nothing . . . The walls which guard the wise man are safe both from flame and assault, they provide no means of entrance—are lofty, impregnable, godlike. Seneca

Our outlook on life, virtue and leadership might be much closer to those of the ancient Greeks and Romans had it not been for the incursion of another tradition—the scandalous world view of a breakaway sect of an irascible people in a remote corner of the Roman Empire. Two figures stand at the head of this social and intellectual incursion: Jesus of Nazareth and Paul of Tarsus.

Reframing the classical tradition

Martin Luther King Jr, like Gandhi before him, built his platform of non-violent leadership and transformation on the words of Jesus to an audience open to armed revolution: 'Blessed are the meek: for they shall inherit the earth' (Matthew 5:5).

The note of social reversal pervades the teachings of Jesus: 'Whoever exalts himself will be humbled, and whoever humbles himself will be exalted' (Matthew 23:12).

At the heart of the Christian explanation of the story of Jesus is the theme of self-sacrifice and humility. As Paul of Tarsus explained the story, Jesus 'humbled himself and became obedient to death' for the benefit of those unable to reciprocate. 'Though he was rich yet for your sake he became poor so that you through his poverty might become rich' (Philippians 2:7–8; 2 Corinthians 8:9). It is a vision that has fired the imagination of artists, writers and leaders over many centuries. Yet it derives from a land, a life and an event deemed ignoble and scandalous by Greeks and Romans.

Paul of Tarsus was a Jewish lawyer and leader, most likely trained in both Jewish and Graeco-Roman law, a fierce opponent of the earliest Christians, and a supporter of terrorism against the occupying Romans. Yet he was soon to become the most articulate advocate of the Christian 'good news'—a term laden with political connotations. ('Good news' was used in announcing the birth of the emperor's son and military victories. Likewise the slogan 'Jesus is Lord' was an affront to 'Caesar is Lord'.) Paul became the architect of what is arguably the most radical reshaping of human relations in Western, if not human, history.

Given what we have seen of the social conventions of Paul's day, consider his innovations and departures from tradition. Palestine had been deeply Hellenised (influenced by Greek culture) for over a century. Jews lived throughout the Roman Empire, many holding positions of high rank. Paul himself was a Roman citizen, an honour passed from forebears who had merited high standing. Paul could play both worlds: zealous Jewish agitator and urbane Hellenised professional. So what would an audience make of his pronouncement that 'there is neither Jew nor Greek, slave nor free, male nor female, for you are all one in Christ Jesus' (Galatians 3:28)? Or when he advised others to 'do nothing out of selfish ambition or vain conceit, but in humility consider others better than yourselves' (Philippians 2:3)? Or to 'not think of yourself more highly than you ought', but to 'associate with people of low position' (Romans 12:3, 16)? Today we prize adaptability. In Paul's world it was unseemly. Grace, he said, drove him to adapt to those he sought to serve. 'I have become all things to all men' (Corinthians 9:19, 22). To most he was unstable and inconstant.

Humility was not an idea to Paul. He would not call it a virtue. It was a commitment, a way of life thrust upon him by his identification with Jesus of Nazareth that he felt compelled to model and to justify. It fed upon his understanding of grace as the new shape of divine and human relations. He took the paramount political metaphor, the body—commonly used to prove the superiority of the head—and used it to teach the equality of all parts and the value of the lowliest. He coined the idea of gifts: that every member was divinely endowed with gifts for service, not personal status. He wrote directly to women, slaves and children, an unparalleled break with convention. He refused to work the crowd with oratory. He declined patronage. He worked with his hands.

If Paul broke with the classical spirit on the virtues, he was no less radical on leadership. He left no room for personal power or office. In a world where leadership was rank, Paul was anti-leadership. This is difficult for us to grasp. He exerted profound influence. He founded communities. He taught and modelled a re-ordering of social relations that would eventually reshape the social order. We are accustomed to calling all of this leadership. Yet he rejected the term. He described himself with simple, demeaning metaphors like slave, servant or gardener. He reframed friendship away from personal gain. In time, the new language (servant) came to delineate rank (minister). But not for Paul.

The intellectual and cultural richness of Western society derives from the tensions, the contradictions, the antagonism and plagiarism between its two great traditions—the classical worlds of the Greeks and Romans, and the Christian world views that grew from Jewish soil. A rich synthesis, made richer by tension and contradiction, was hammered out over four centuries. This conflation has shaped our expectations of leadership. We seek a man or woman of strong intellect and vision to build the *polis*. We want leaders made worthy by grace and humility, not rank. We desire leadership that upholds the ideals of democracy, but democracy does not mean to us what it meant to the ancient Greeks. We desire virtues of compassion and humility in our leaders, but the early sources of these qualities are found in New Testament letters hostile to leadership.

Westerners live in multicultural societies that bear witness to two traditions above all others. We may not have read Aristotle, nor hold Christian convictions, but we have inherited their richly contradictory notions and practices of virtue, leadership and humility. In this creative tension we seek an understanding and practice of humility for own times.

On humility

The *Concise Macquarie Dictionary* defines humility as:

Humility: *The quality of being humble; (a) modest sense of one's own significance.*

It is akin to modesty, which the *Oxford Dictionary* defines as that disposition of 'a moderate or humble estimate of one's merits, importance, etc.; free from vanity, egotism, boastfulness, or great pretensions . . . free from ostentation or showy extravagance'.

In colloquial speech, Australians talk about 'eating humble pie', 'eating crow', 'not getting above oneself', 'not being up yourself', being 'happy to take a back seat' and 'not putting yourself forward'. We refer affectionately or sympathetically to unpretentious (and usually struggling or unsuccessful) people as 'battlers' or 'underdogs'. A man, sometimes a woman, may refer to his or her spouse as 'the better half'. Our distaste for arrogance and unreasonable pride is captured in sayings like 'she doesn't suffer fools', 'he's up himself', 'she's got a healthy ego', 'he's got tickets on himself' and 'she thinks she's the ants pants'. We don't like those who 'big note' themselves. Somehow we have maintained this preference for humility and distaste for arrogance in the face of the rampant self-promotion of marketing and media spin-doctors.

'Humility,' Rabbi Jonathan Sacks maintains, 'is the orphaned virtue of our age':

Its demise came with the threatening anonymity of mass culture alongside the loss of neighborhoods and congregations. Today's creed is, 'If you've got it, flaunt it.' Humility, being humble, didn't stand a chance. What a shame . . . True virtue never needs to advertise itself. That is why I find the aggressive packaging of personality so sad. It speaks of loneliness, the profound, endemic loneliness of a world without relationships of fidelity and trust.

Is humility weakness? Executives have said to me: 'If I practice humility it will be interpreted as weakness. Surely it *is* a weakness if I miss out on some reward or recognition by putting others forward.' If by 'strength' we mean putting ourselves in a stronger position *for ourselves*—in other words, personal gain—then, yes, humility *is* weakness. Indeed, this is why humility did *not* appear as a virtue, human or divine, in ancient Greece and Rome. Humility *will be* weakness in any social system that values status over substance, personality over character, and performance over depth. The path of humility *is* social weakness. It is to refuse the games and cop the possible flak. So is humility just for 'mugs', for those who aren't smart enough to play the game?

I think it depends first on our view of strength, and second on the size of our world. To lead humbly is to accept rank but to use it on behalf of others. To lead humbly is to refuse status. This is strength—*strength of character*. This is the strength of one whose world is bigger than his or her ego. This is the strength that enables a leader to pursue a noble dream in a noble way.

On building what is truly great

I have to confess I'm no fan of management books. But recently I read one that had me cheering. Jim Collins's *Good to Great* is the sequel to the well-known *Built to Last*, which he co-authored with Jerry Porras. In *Built to Last*, Collins and Porras wanted to know which corporations had truly lasted. They made a study of corporations that passed a battery of intimidating tests of reputation, product quality, market share and financial performance, and had done so for over 50 years. In *Good to Great*, Jim Collins and his team pursued a different question: 'Can a good company become a great company, and if so, how?' The team began with 1435 companies, gradually developing robust and exacting criteria and narrowing the list to 11 companies they believed were truly great and 11 direct comparison companies who had achieved success but never greatness.

Well into the research, the team began to report that leaders of the 11 great companies showed different traits to their counterparts. What is crucial here is that Collins did *not* set out to create a new theory of leadership. He explicitly warned the team against this.

I gave the research team explicit instructions to downplay *the role of top executives so that we would avoid the simplistic 'credit the teacher' or 'blame the leader' thinking . . . I kept insisting 'Ignore the executives'. But the research team kept pushing back, 'No! There is something consistently unusual about them. We can't ignore them' . . . Finally, . . . the data won.*

The data showed an uncanny inverse image between the leaders of the great companies and their direct comparisons (see table 1.1).

Two words summed up what Collins and his team believed they had seen in these leaders of truly great companies: *humility + will*.

The argument for humility will mean little to those whose focus is on the short term and their own advancement. If the daily movement of the share price is our guide to significance, then we shouldn't bother with humility. Arrogance, bravado and a certain callousness in the use of people will get the results—for as long as they last. By comparison, building what lasts requires faith,

Table 1.1: The traits of great leaders

The comparison leaders	The great leaders
Mostly outside appointments	Almost all long-term employees
Attained high public profile. Turnaround of the company widely featured in the media.	Relatively unknown. Turnaround stories had comparatively modest publicity.
Explained success by looking in the mirror.	Explained success by looking out of the window.
Explained failure and setbacks by looking out of the window.	Explained failure and setbacks by looking in the mirror.
Gung-ho enthusiasts.	Often modest and adverse to attention.
Ambitious for their own careers.	Ambitious for what they were building.

persistence, resolve and grace. Humility opens us to a world big enough to warrant perseverance and big enough to learn from. Humility is only for those who wish to build something great, something that lasts, something noble. Think of the recent corporate collapses in both Australia and the USA. Think of the leaders. Humility?

Do the big names need humility or will it just get in the road? It comes down to the breadth and depth of our view of life. What seems great may in truth be small; what seems small may be great. To quote the good Rabbi once more:

> *What a glorious revelation humility is of the human spirit . . . True humility is one of the most life-enhancing of all virtues. It does not mean undervaluing or underestimating yourself. It means valuing other people. It signals an openness to life's grandeur and the willingness to be surprised, uplifted, by goodness wherever one finds it . . . False humility is the pretence that one is small. True humility is the consciousness of standing in the presence of greatness.* Jonathon Sacks

Cynicism has no comeback to humility. It will mock but it has no answer. Cynicism is a sickly, small view of the world. A world where people do not change. Where nothing noble can be done. Where no-one can act for the good of others. Where there is no joy in learning and making. Sacks is right: 'Humility opens us to the world.'

Humility is the heart of an inquiring mind. The world is big. I am big. No point denying it. No bigger than others, and no smaller. Just big and different. Life holds infinite mysteries and joys. I can learn them only if I don't think I already know. Only if I don't think *you* can't teach me.

Humility is a door to wisdom—to reading ourselves, others and the world around us with insight. The wise leader prizes the gaining of wisdom above all else. In the words of an ancient chief executive: 'Wisdom is supreme; therefore get wisdom. Though it cost you all you have, get understanding' (Proverbs 4:7). Those who would learn to lead wisely must receive and give instruction humbly:

Yu, shall I tell you what it is to know? To say you know when you know, and to say you do not when you do not, that is knowledge.   Confucius

The way of a fool seems right to him, but a wise man listens to advice . . . A mocker resents correction; he will not consult the wise . . . He who listens to a life-giving rebuke will be at home among the wise.

Proverbs 12:15; 15:12, 31

There is paradox in what we are saying about humility. To be humble is to recognise that we are both small and big. Small in the face of a big world offering a large life. Big in the face of the petty fears and self-doubt that may rob us of the joy of life. Small as those who have much to learn. Big as those who can learn far more than we can imagine. Small as a child helpless in his mother's arms. Big as a child who brings a father to his knees. If we are indeed fearfully and wonderfully made, then humility is our amen.

A commitment to life

In the film *Dead Poets' Society*, the Robin Williams character, English teacher John Keating, takes his new charges into the school foyer for their first class. He has them read a poem that begins: 'Gather ye rose buds while ye may, while time is still a-flying'. 'The Latin term for this sentiment,' he explains, 'is *carpe diem* . . . seize the day!' Drawing them close to photos of long dead graduates, he breathes the paradox: 'They are food for worms lads . . . Make your lives extraordinary.' You will die; so live. This is no simple 'make the most of what you have' speech. Later he has them rip out the introduction in their textbooks—not just because it gives the wrong idea of poetry, but because it offers a false orientation to life, to which poetry is a door, a key, a window.

The character John Keating seizes on the extraordinary power of death to orient the heart and mind. It is a truth found in many traditions:

One who is a Samurai must before all things keep constantly before him, by day and by night, the fact that he must die.   Yâuzan Daidâoji

---

Drawing on the work of the German philosopher Heidegger, William Barrett wrote:

Men die. This happens every day in the world. Death is a public event in the world, of which we take notice in obituaries . . . But so long as death remains a fact outside ourselves, we have not yet passed from the proposition 'Men die' to the proposition 'I am to die' . . . The authentic meaning of death—'I am to die'—is not an external and public fact within the world, but an internal possibility of my own Being . . . Only by taking my death into myself, according to Heidegger, does an authentic existence become possible for me . . . Though terrifying, the taking of death into ourselves is also liberating. It frees us from servitude to the petty cares that threaten to engulf our daily life and thereby opens us to the essential projects by which we can make our lives personally and significantly our own.

Humility is a commitment to life when the certainty of our own death loses its fear. We *will* die. So what lasts? What is it to live meaningfully? What gives meaning to our lives? Memories. Relationships. The joy of intimacy and the meeting of minds. Making. The bringing to existence of what would not have been except for us. The memories of what we have created with, and on behalf of, others.

It is crucial that we not see humility as synonymous with being shy, withdrawn, quiet, self-effacing or self-critical. There is nothing wrong with any of these behaviours. But they must not define humility. Humility is as much at home among the gregarious, ambitious and confident. Humility is not being negative about ourselves. Negativity poisons humility with self-pity and self-centredness. In my experience many people struggle with this very point. Can I value my abilities and myself without becoming arrogant?

A couple of years ago I was leading a small design team for a client organisation and had taken them away to workshop the skills of strategic conversation and design. As part of the workshop, I had the team complete an exercise individually and then meet up with a partner to talk through the insights they gained. The exercise works from a simple analogy. In many ball sports we speak of sweet spots—that place on the club, bat or racquet from which the ball flies strong and true. By extension we speak of those moments when everything comes together beautifully. We all experience sweet spots and not just in sports. I asked the team to find a quiet place and map the sweet spots in their lives. The moments when they knew they were doing what they loved, what they were good at, and what was of value to others. Some moments contain only one of these; some contain all.

Several team members were rising stars and obvious choices. One was not. Her supervisors had been taken aback when I had said I wanted to invite her onto the team. She had limited education, no professional qualifications, and was in a low-paid position. But I had witnessed her insight, integrity and earthy manner of getting to the heart of things. Unknown to the rest of us, she found the exercise paralysing. 'I have never stopped to think positively about myself,' she told us later. 'I couldn't think of anything.' Her partner for the exercise was a gentle man of great depth. When he found her she was feeling blank and stupid. An hour later she had told him story after story of remarkable personal growth through difficulties, employment initiatives, small business ventures and community involvements. We were stunned by the tapestry he had mapped of her stories and the emerging portrait of her character and competence. Late that night we spoke at length. She was startled by glimpses of unforeseen meaning and possibility.

A few months later she participated with senior leaders from many organisations in a development workshop run by a colleague of mine. I dropped by on the last day, quietly taking my place at the rear of the room. With great skill she was leading a group of senior executives to new clarity about a pressing problem. The original workshop was a watershed for her. She now saw herself as competent and successful, with skills far beyond her position. Did this confidence kill humility? On the contrary. What she displayed before was more negativity than humility. Her sense of unworthiness capped her capacity to learn and to draw out the insights of others. Her joy now is to use her gifts to help others find uncommon clarity. *That* is humility.

Learning humility

So can humility be taught? By a program, no. By life, yes. At the end of a *Good to Great* seminar, Jim Collins was asked if a person can learn to be a great leader, a leader characterised by humility and will—what he calls a 'level 5 leader'. His response? 'A "Ten-Step List to Level 5" would trivialise the concept.'

No program teaches greatness. How do I learn patience? How do I learn to love? How do I learn humility? By pain and joy and being open to uncertainty. More than programs, we need conversations that provoke us to:

1. Focus on character more than personality. Character, it has been said, is what we are in the dark.
2. Watch and emulate those whose characters impress us as much or more than their achievements.

There is no point in seeking the views of a Gentleman who, though he sets his heart on the Way, is ashamed of poor food and poor clothes.

Confucius

---

3. Find people who will tell us the truth—mentors who will challenge us to live humbly and nobly.

Hui is no help to me at all. He is pleased with everything I say.

Confucius

4. Face our mistakes.

Go and humble yourself; press your plea with your neighbour.

Proverbs 6:3

5. Refuse to lay guilt trips on people. Think of what we do with plans and performance reviews—are they just wish lists and guilt sheets?
6. Lift up others. Extend kindness and dignity to others without thought to their merit or status or to our own.
7. Take time to enjoy life and other people deeply.
8. Mentor generously. Mentor the rising stars. Mentor also those deemed less likely.
9. Speak with intent.

The tongue that brings healing is a tree of life, but a deceitful tongue crushes the spirit. Proverbs 15:4

10. Nurture moral imagination to sense the consequences of our decisions and actions.
11. Challenge ourselves with three little words: 'On behalf of' whom or what will this make a difference?
12. Avoid creating false dilemmas. We can be humble and confident; modest and sure of our gifts and talents. Ultimately, humility is not shaped by how we regard ourselves, but by how we regard others.
13. Avoid becoming paralysed by motives. Life and leadership is not as neat as our seven virtues. Humility comes wrapped in stories, self-perceptions and expectations. There are no pure motives. The test is openness to genuine conversation.
14. Face anxiety. Leadership involves tough choices. We cannot know how our choices will turn out until we choose. This

creates anxiety. Anxiety puts us on a knife-edge: to face it and grow, or run away and regress.

15. Refuse to protect ourselves with petty behaviour. No gossip. No put-downs in front of colleagues. No thinly disguised references to others.

16. Not always insist on our rights and entitlements. Imagine a seeming deadlock between our group and another. We can insist that the other group provide the service they have promised. Or we can acknowledge that they need our input. We can then lift the monkey off their backs—and our own.

17. Give up on the myth of control by giving up on formulas for leading people.

18. Not fish for compliments.

It is not the failure of others to appreciate your abilities that should trouble you, but rather your failure to appreciate theirs.   Confucius

---

19. Let go of ideals and stereotypes about leadership. There is no one pattern to greatness.

Humility comes before honour.   Proverbs 15:33

These 19 points are not the answer to everything. On another day I may have come up with 12 or 27. Every reader can think of their own points to add. We are simply reflecting on life as we know it. Life—where we stuff up, succeed and sometimes learn.

I learned three wonderful little aphorisms from my father that have come back to me time and again. I do not know their original sources. Most likely you have heard them before:

Take care in little things.
Faithful in little things, faithful in big things.
Leave things/people better than you found them.

He was trying to inculcate in me a sense of the beauty in humility and love. No task or person is insignificant. The measure of character is what we do when no-one is watching; when the task is too small for others to notice. If we want to be given large responsibilities and opportunities, then we must earn the privilege

through discharging smaller responsibilities well. The test comes
when we are accustomed to bigger things. What happens when we
are asked to do something small? Many of us were taught to leave
things better than we found them, like filling up with petrol before
we return our friend's car. My dad tried to teach me that this was as
true of people as cars. There's a knife-edge there. To think of
'leaving people better than we found them' can smack of
patronising and claiming to know better. That wasn't his intent.
It was simply the thoughtfulness to speak a word that might
encourage, a word that might open the door to a bigger world
for others.

Humility and other virtues and qualities

Humility needs to be seen in relationship to our other virtues and
qualities. It is inward looking in a way most other virtues are not.
Humility is a stance I take towards myself before it is a stance I
take towards others. With the possible exception of integrity, the
other virtues are mostly a stance we take towards others and the
wider challenges of life. I'm not saying that humility is the most
important. The virtues need to be seen as interdependent. Each
needs to be seen in the light of the others. Humility without
compassion, courage or integrity is hollow. Without humility the
other virtues may become parodies:

- Compassion without humility is likely to be patronising.
- Courage without humility is likely to be foolhardy.
- Humour without humility is likely to be cruel.
- Integrity without humility is likely to be self-righteous.
- Passion without humility is likely to be overbearing.
- Wisdom without humility is likely to be pompous.

In *On Equilibrium*, John Ralston Saul makes a case for the
combined use of six universal qualities as our primary means of
ensuring the good of the *polis*, what Aristotle called the
'partnership in living well'. We might argue over his distinctions
between virtues, values, qualities and characteristics. We may argue
over his final choice of the six qualities. What he offers, though, is
a rich view of what is common to us all, but not always common
in use. Each quality is made richer and surer by humility:

1. Humility exalts common sense—it challenges the tyranny of experts.
2. Humility brings a human face to ethics—it brings abstraction back to earth.
3. Humility fires imagination—it silences cynicism and takes vision beyond us.
4. Humility enlightens intuition—it deepens discernment.
5. Humility is the straight edge of memory—it checks the distortions of self-interest.
6. Humility makes reason reasonable—it teaches us to value clear thinking as nothing more or less than that.

On humility with nobility

Clearly, humility does not exist in isolation from the other virtues, qualities and arts of leadership. When it comes to leadership there is perhaps one characteristic manner of being that stands out as the natural twin of humility. Humility and nobility. Humility *with* nobility:

Honor is not the same as public acclaim. Virtue is not determined in moments of public attention to our behavior. Courage, devotion, compassion, humility—all the noble human qualities—are not practiced in pursuit of public approval. They are means to much nobler ends. And they are ends in themselves.   Senator John McCain

---

According to the *Concise Macquarie Dictionary*, to be noble is to be:

Admirable in dignity of conception, or in manner of expression, execution, or composition; imposing in appearance; stately; magnificent; of an admirably high quality.

We are not talking about nobility in the sense of ranks made elite by birth or decree, but of nobility of *purpose*, and of a personal bearing that befits that purpose.

Joshua Chamberlain

Humility with nobility is easier to see than to define.

The telemovie *Gettysburg* depicts the devastating American Civil War battle near the town of the same name. It is based on the well-researched Pulitzer Prize novel, *Killer Angels* by Michael Shaara. The story is as follows:

It is 1863. Colonel Joshua 'Lawrence' Chamberlain has taken command of the 20th Maine regiment, now reduced from 1000 men to less than 300, and 120 men of the now disbanded 2nd Maine are arriving under guard. They have refused to fight. Most soldiers enlisted for two years. These men signed for three years but thought they signed to fight with the 2nd Maine only. When the regiment disbanded, they believed they were free to go home but found they had to serve one more year. They mutinied. Chamberlain is 'authorised to shoot any man who will not do his duty'. A spiteful young captain has marched them at bayonet point and without food in order to 'break them'. When dismissed, he seeks to humiliate them one last time.

Chamberlain dismisses the guards. He provides food and shelter. In a brief exchange, Private Buckland identifies himself as the elected spokesman for the mutineers. Chamberlain invites Buckland to his shelter, where Buckland recounts the men's grievances. A courier announces that the 20th Maine must move immediately to the forward position. Buckland leaves, and after a delay, Chamberlain gathers the mutineers to address them.

He begins awkwardly, explaining that his new orders give them little time to talk. He comes clean: 'They tell me I can shoot you. Well, we both know I won't do that. Maybe someone else will, but I won't.' His passion grows as he speaks. They enlisted to fight for many reasons; mostly, they thought it was the right thing to do. He sees a noble purpose: 'We are an army out to set other men free.' He is heavy with war: 'We have all seen men die.' Climaxing his impromptu speech, the former professor of rhetoric becomes self-conscious and awkward: 'Sorry, I didn't mean to preach.' He offers muskets to any man who will fight and gives his word that 'nothing more will be said by anyone anywhere'. For those who refuse to fight he promises to see they get a fair trial. He pauses: 'Gentlemen, I think if we lose this fight, we lose the war. So if you choose to join us, I'll be personally very grateful.'

Chamberlain's humility and nobility impresses and inspires. He will not tolerate the captain's disrespect, neither of himself nor of the mutineers. His first words are to dismiss the guards. He looks to the mutineers' wellbeing. Buckland is taken aback, first by Chamberlain's invitation, then by the offer of his hand, coffee and a seat. Chamberlain sits quietly while Buckland denounces 'these officers, these gentlemen . . . these lame-brained bastards from West Point'. (Australian soldiers suffering under incompetent English officers at Gallipoli in World War One would have understood.) Chamberlain had not been to West Point. He was a professor. He does not distance himself, nor take exception, but quietly reads the courage in the awkward private.

Walking to address the men he is unsure of what to do. He stands below them and makes no attempt to call them to formal order. He acknowledges Buckland. He believes he owes the men a reason. He feels strongly about the war, notwithstanding the uncertainty and confusion that will grow within him later. He sums up in story where they find themselves. It is truthful and unpromising. He paints a picture of what they are fighting for. He is clear about their choices. He cannot make them fight. He won't shoot them. They will be coming. He will get them a fair trial. He neither deceives nor withholds knowledge that is rightfully theirs. He apologises for 'preaching'. He calls them 'gentlemen'.

Humility and nobility. One man among others. Aware of his relative inexperience. Courteous and dignifying. Cutting vitriol short. Holding his position with honour. Willing to listen and learn. Giving a man a chance to prove himself. Looking beyond the outburst. No wounded pride. He speaks without affectation. He respects their anger and grief. He offers only what he can. He attempts to lift their hearts and minds to what he believes is a noble purpose.

Of the 120 mutineers, 114 men chose that day to fight. Days later he appealed again to the final six, three of whom fought. One may have saved Chamberlain's life. The three remaining mutineers received a fair trial. No action was taken against the others. Chamberlain's actions at Gettysburg turned the battle. He was gravely wounded in later battles, and promoted to Major General. Chosen by General Grant to receive the Southern surrender at Appomattox, he stunned both sides by calling his troops to salute the defeated Southerners. He was elected Governor of Maine four times, and finally succumbed to his war wounds in 1914. His men held him in awe and devotion to the end.

'Weary' Dunlop

Closer to home I think of Captain Edward 'Weary' Dunlop and his indefatigable labours as the senior medical officer and sometimes commanding officer among Australian prisoners of war in Burma during the Second World War. Weary is remembered for many things. His brilliant surgical innovations first performed with bamboo and other improvised instruments and aids; his fearless confrontation and gentle wooing of the Japanese guards and officers to win relief and supplies for his men wherever possible; his distaste at the vengeful treatment of many former guards after the Japanese surrender; and his tireless work for all returned POWs and their families until his death.

When he resumed his surgical career in Australia, some peers were jealous of the goodwill shown to him. They sought to taint his efforts on behalf of others with the smear of mixed motives. His biographer, Sue Ebury, recounts Weary's own explanation:

Hintok 1943 is the key, when he read the Sermon on the Mount in the midst of 'all the misery, the squalor, the grey rain and slush and sick and dying people'. He had never felt more useful. It was then that he was possessed by a 'marvellous, almost religious experience . . . a sort of happiness. I understood what it would mean to love your neighbour more than yourself'.

Evelyn Crawford

Evelyn Crawford lived a truly 'remarkable life'. She didn't know it at the time, but a noble dream began to form in the heart and mind of this young Aboriginal girl from her earliest days growing up in far north-western New South Wales and south-eastern Queensland in the 1930s. A vision of life made better by wisdom and education wherever it could be found. Her grandparents bequeathed to her a deep appreciation for the wisdom and vast knowledge of those who live close to the land. She learned to see beyond. She learned to master complex languages and custom. From her first school teacher she learned that education was a door to a different life. At the white man's tip outside of town she found labels and discarded papers holding precious words to learn to read and write. At the mission school she encountered for the first time the prejudice and ignorance that only deepened her resolve to bring the kinds of learning that would reconcile people. As she relates in her autobiography, *Over My Tracks: A Remarkable Life*, her dream took forty years to begin to realise:

We had no idea what our little group, three Aboriginal women and one white man, would become in later years. We were just thinking—at least I was—from one week to another. It wasn't anything pre-planned. We never said, 'If we get this done, we can surely get that done.' We just went ahead very, very slowly . . . We knew that if we wanted to be in the education system, and get other people to come forward and do the same thing after us, we'd have to work bloody hard to get in, and to be accepted, because we started from scratch. The challenge was there for me, an old woman almost fifty, and I never, ever walked away from a challenge in my life.

With several friends and colleagues, Evelyn Crawford was at the forefront of establishing a place for Aboriginal teachers' aides in public schools; technical college classes for Aborigines; an Aboriginal liaison department in the New South Wales public education system; and, finally, full teacher training and benefits for Aboriginal teachers. Through it all she tended to play down her own capabilities and ignored her own rights while working tirelessly to applaud the talents and protect the rights of others. She summed up herself well: 'Yes, we were the gate openers, and I'm proud of the ones that come through that gate.' Nobility with humility.

On letting tall poppies grow

One hundred remarkable young adults had gathered in the town of Launceston to 'pass through a gate' at the Future Leaders Forum sponsored by the Foundation for Young Australians. One hundred chosen from hundreds of nominations from around Australia. For six days they listened to politicians, chief executives, economists, environmentalists, activists, academics and social researchers addressing the question: 'What will you face as a leader in this country in the next 10 or 20 years?' Between sessions they worked in small groups, framing their own pictures of the society they hoped to leave to their children. On the last day I met with them to address the question: 'What will it take for you to make a difference?'

This was an impressive group. The most diverse I have ever seen in terms of gender, ethnicity, race, religion, education, work, socio-economic background, interests and achievements. Many already had a significant public profile. I began my session with two questions.

'After six heady days,' I asked, 'how many of you are awed at your new colleagues and think to yourself, "What am I doing here?"' Almost every hand went up. 'And how many of you,' I continued, 'have parents, siblings, friends and colleagues who can't quite fathom why you would spend a week in a conference like this, and you struggle to know how to tell them because you feel somewhat awkward, even embarrassed, to talk about it?' Once again, almost every hand went up.

Most of these 100 highly talented, motivated, articulate, high achieving, highly regarded young Australian adults indicated that they felt anxious and awkward about saying they wanted to make a difference. They didn't lack drive, passion or vision. There were some very healthy egos. What they felt was anticipation. They anticipated a disposition among Australians that stands ready to cut down those who stand tall.

In his book, *Turning Point: Australians Choosing their Future*, Hugh Mackay comments on the so-called tall poppy syndrome:

It's not the tall poppies we slash: it's the one's that act tall. So, to the list of other desirable attributes in a leader—strength, integrity, passion— we must add the important modifier: humility. With humility, strength can be expressed with dignity and grace; integrity can be assumed, without anyone's attention being drawn to it; passion can be focused on the task at hand, without spilling over into lust for power. (Some older Australians recall Curtin and Chifley—as some older Americans recall Truman—as leaders who displayed true humility.)

Australians do hate arrogance. But passion is not arrogance. Nobility is not elitism. Humility is not self-deprecation. Perhaps we have little deep understanding of humility or nobility. We seem embarrassed by passion; awkward about a truly noble cause. Thus we cut down those who have a dream and dare to realise it.

We do need to check arrogance. But we also need to encourage the strength of character, the robustness, to care deeply and to commit to making a difference. Humility does not negate passion, commitment or confidence; it makes them credible.

A few months after my Tasmanian experience, the Foundation for Young Australians invited me to speak with 100 teenagers chosen from public and private schools across Australia. The Centenary of Federation was in 2001 and these young people were our Federation Envoys, telling the story of Federation in their schools and communities. They had gathered at Parliament House, Canberra, for a final debrief. Deciding against a formal speech, we found a large corridor where the young people sat on the ground leaving a path for me to wander as I spoke with them. As with their older counterparts, I began by asking them questions.

'When you applied a year ago to become a Federation Envoy,' I asked, 'did you think then that you were able to make a difference in any of the serious issues that face your communities?' Almost all were negative. 'What about now?' I inquired. 'Do you think you can make a difference now?' Almost all were positive. 'So what has happened for you in this past year?' I added. They began to tell stories. Initiatives they had taken. Conversations that had changed them and changed others. A growing confidence. Some demurred. The exchange was fascinating.

I passed around copies of a piece of writing by Marianne Williamson, which was quoted by Nelson Mandela in his 1994 speech on being inaugurated as President of South Africa:

Our deepest fear is not that we are inadequate. Our deepest fear is that we are powerful beyond measure. It is our light, not our darkness, that most frightens us. We ask ourselves, 'Who am I to be brilliant?' Actually, who are you not to be? You are a child of God. Your playing small does not serve the world. There is nothing enlightened about shrinking, so that other people won't feel insecure around you. We were born to make manifest the glory of God that is within us. It is not just in some of us, it's in everyone and, as we let our own light shine, we unconsciously give other people the permission to do the same. As we are liberated from our fear, our presence automatically liberates others.

It is not humility that makes us shrink back. It is not arrogant to commit to being as brilliant, as big, as glorious, as unafraid as possible. With Williamson's poem, and his own life, Mandela moved South Africa and us all to grasp humility with nobility. Whatever the man's flaws, he modelled it for us. The young people grasped this. They spoke of the fear that holds them back. They spoke of peers who tried to hold them back. They voiced the desire to hang on to desire—the desire to make a difference.

Conclusion

Recall our new CEO. She ponders this call to lead wisely. It resonates with her common sense, ethics, imagination, intuition, memory and reason. People are not resources to be managed. She will not manage her way to building what is truly great. Instead, she and many others must *lead*. The *polis* of Aristotle's *Politics*, the 'partnership in living well', confronts her with the call to virtue. Courage, justice, self-control and wisdom. Each makes their claim upon her. But she hears another call too. To grace and compassion and humility. Rank is but a context . . . status has no place . . . the conservatism of Aristotle and Seneca is unsettled by the radicalism of Jesus and Paul. She seeks humility with nobility. Singleness of purpose to build what truly matters. Clarity to focus on one or two crucial challenges. Deep respect for all. Openness to learn from everyone. The channelling of ego into what they will build.

Looking out the window at a neighbouring construction site, an image forms in her mind. Aristotle wanted the leaders of Athens to build a 'partnership in living well'. Paul inverted contemporary political metaphors to teach the equality and dignity of all. Jim Collins seeks to understand the minds and hearts of those who build what is truly great. The image she sees comes into focus.

Leading is like bricklaying. We have a picture of the *polis* in our minds. What emerges is close but never exact. We learn to set a string line and work the level. But it's the eye that grows to know what's plumb and true—the arts of leadership.

Then there's the mortar, the 'mud'. The qualities. The virtues. Humility. Nobility. Courage. Compassion. Integrity. All of them. Bricklayers don't skimp on mud. They don't measure it out. They throw it on. Extravagantly. And so it is with leaders who build what is great.

Everyone has dignity. We call some kids gifted and talented. But they're *all* gifted and talented. Everyone. Each person at each desk, building site, office, machine, headset and driver's wheel is gifted and talented. Some see it. Some don't. What could we create if we made the space for people to bring the very best of what they have to all that they do? Arrogance, rudeness and indifference make the world smaller.

Humility with nobility opens up a bigger life. Ambition directed into what we build. A willingness to learn from all. An idea that inspires and is open to question. A willingness to do little things well. Bringing dignity to a role without superiority. Graciousness when shown we are wrong. Making sure praise goes to those who deserve it.

I have three precious things which I hold fast and prize. The first is gentleness; the second frugality; the third is humility, which keeps me from putting myself before others. Be gentle and you can be bold; be frugal and you can be liberal; avoid putting yourself before others and you can become a leader among men.   Lao Tzu

---

Humility is the mud with which we build partnerships in living well. Be extravagant with it.

Humility with nobility

Here are seven sayings that urge me to live beyond my pettiness. Some are old friends; some new. They offer no program. No easy answers. They are worthy of deep reflection.

1 'When a man intermingles praise of himself with censure of another, and causes another's disgrace to secure glory for himself, he is altogether odious and vulgar, as one who would win applause from the humiliation of another.'   *Plutarch*

2 'Whoever exalts himself will be humbled, and whoever humbles himself will be exalted.'   *Jesus*

3 'Therefore, desiring to rule over the people, one must in one's words humble oneself before them; and, desiring to lead the people, one must, in one's person, follow behind them.' *Lao Tzu*

---

4 'Do not think of yourself more highly than you ought, but think of yourself with sober judgement.' *Paul* in Romans 12:3

5 '[The sage] does not show himself, and so is conspicuous; he does not consider himself right, and so is illustrious; he does not brag, and so has merit; he does not boast, and so endures.'

Lao Tzu

6 'Great joys come from contemplating noble works.' *Democritus*

7 'Humility is the orphaned virtue of our age.'

Rabbi Jonathan Sacks

For further exploration

—Aristotle, *Politics*, Penguin, London, 1962.

Aristotle's teacher, Plato, wrote the *Republic* to argue for the supremacy of a city in which all know their place and act exactly according to it. Aristotle believed diversity made the city vibrant and sustainable. *Politics* makes his case.

—Jim Collins, *Good to Great*, Harper Business, New York, 2001.

At last, a management book that looks beyond the hype. A great read grounded in careful research. (Someone needs to do the same work on Australian corporations.) Don't let the 'level 5 leader' tag distract you from the book's good sense.

—Evelyn Crawford, *Over My Tracks: A Remarkable Life*, Penguin, Melbourne, 1993.

A wonderful story. My work with public education underscores to me the debt we owe those who teach our children well and lead our schools wisely. Evelyn Crawford was a pioneer for all kids.

—David Day, *John Curtin: A Life*, Harper Collins, Sydney, 1999.

Great read about a fascinating life. Curtin was a reluctant and unlikely Prime Minister who rose to the occasion when Australia needed him most during the Second World War.

—Sue Ebury, *Weary: The Life of Sir Edward Dunlop*, Penguin, Melbourne, 1995.

Why has no-one made a film from this book? One of the great stories of selflessness for a noble cause in the most appalling circumstances.

—Lao Tzu, *Tao de Ching*, Penguin, London, 1963.
  The classic enigmatic Eastern sage. Don't look for systems, processes or easy answers. His cryptic sayings are tantalisingly insightful (and occasionally slightly batty).
—Tom Morris, *True Success: A New Philosophy of Excellence*, Berkeley, New York, 1995.
  Like no other success book. Just what you'd expect from an undergraduate business student and rock guitarist who became America's favourite philosophy professor and the Disney spokesman for Winnie the Pooh. Full of great good sense.
—Paul's Letter to the Philippians, *New Testament*, any edition.
  Contains many of the key sayings, examples and arguments that began the subversion of the classical assumption of virtue and leadership as tied to rank. Startling self-awareness.
—Plutarch, 'How to tell a flatterer from a friend', in *Essays*, Penguin, London, 1992.
  The best of the tender classical conscience about flattery and self-praise. Lays the ground on which subsequent Christian thinkers found room for a synthesis of the two world views.
—John Ralston Saul, *On Equilibrium*, Penguin, London, 2001.
  A significant book. Argues that the good of society requires the integrated use of the six common human qualities: common sense, ethics, imagination, intuition, memory and reason. Stinging and generally well-targeted critique of managerialism.
—Rabbi Jonathan Sacks, *Humility, An Endangered Virtue*, at www.jewish-holiday.com/humvirtue.html.
  Delightful read. This has to redeem at least a few thousand worthless articles on the Net.
—Mark Strom, 'Character, wisdom, and being a leader', in *Foundation for Young Australians Conference Papers*, Launceston, 2001.
  Provides an introduction to my understanding of story, design, promise and grace as the arts of leading wisely.

COURAGE

2

Ray Weekes

About the author

Ray Weekes, BCom UNSW, Grad Dip Bus Admin UNSW, Grad Dip Ed USyd, ACA, FAICD, FAIM

Ray Weekes is a Brisbane-based business leader. He is Chairman of the Brisbane Institute, CEO-in-Residence/Adjunct Professor in the Faculty of Business at the Queensland University of Technology, and a director of the Pacific Film and Television Commission and other companies. He is also an adviser to various companies, a Member of the Institute of Chartered Accountants in Australia and a Fellow of the Australian Institute of Company Directors.

He was formerly the Chief Executive and Executive Director of the major multi-national company Rothmans Holdings Limited, Chief Executive of Rothmans New Zealand and Managing Director of the globally recognised Castlemaine Perkins Ltd (makers of XXXX beer). As Chief Executive Officer of Rothmans Holdings Limited, he was responsible for the performance of group operations in Australia, New Zealand, Indonesia, the Philippines, Papua New Guinea, Fiji, Western Samoa and various South Pacific territories. The group had in excess of 5000 personnel.

Throughout his senior executive career, Ray has continued to explore the leadership practices that truly work in organisations. Of particular importance to him is how companies develop and align their people.

Ray is a highly regarded speaker on leadership and management issues and is a Fellow of the Australian Institute of Management.

Ray Weekes can be reached at rayweekes@aol.com.

Introduction

It was Tom Peters, in an article on what makes a successful leader, who concluded that great leaders are frighteningly smart, have tons of animal energy, are blessed with monumental impatience, are able to distil a vision for their troops, and can recognise and resolve the big issues. They maintain a healthy disgust for bureaucracy, are performance freaks, are honest and straightforward straight-shooters, are rapidly decisive, are future focused and not report or past oriented. Great leaders are also rigorous in their own execution and follow-up and are highly driven.

This individual leader exists largely in Tom Peters's imagination.

Realistically, a leader can be some of those things all of the time and all of those things some of the time. But one of the true virtues of leadership that is missing from Tom's rather colourful list is *courage*. This was recognised by Chief of the Defence Force, Major General Peter Cosgrove, in an address on his leadership experiences to the QUT Business Leaders' Forum in 2000. He listed four essential elements of leadership: integrity, humility, compassion and courage; with courage having the subsets of physical and moral courage.

It is moral courage (as opposed to physical courage), and its relationship to leadership, that this chapter will examine. The stories told and the lessons drawn will be from today's business world, and seen from an Australian perspective (but the discussion could just as easily apply to leadership in the seventeenth century, or in China, or in the realm of politics—these are universal themes).

What is courage?

Lord Moran defined courage as:

The quality of mind which enables one to encounter danger and difficulties with firmness, or without fear, or fainting of heart . . . and a . . . firmness of spirit that faces danger or extreme difficulty without flinching or retreating.

The heroic US General William T Sherman defined courage as 'a perfect sensibility of the measure of danger and a mental willingness to endure it'. Courage is founded on a certain imagination, self-awareness and well-considered fear.

Mark Twain said that: 'Courage is resistance to fear, mastery of fear—not absence of fear.' In other words, for there to be courage, you have to be doing what you're afraid to do.

For the Greek philosophers, courage was one of the cardinal virtues. Plato believed that courage, both physical and moral, needed to be combined with the other virtues (wisdom, temperance and justice) or it could be misused. He said that courage was 'strength of purpose directed at the right object and in the right context'. It enabled resistance to fear, pain and the temptations of pleasure. For Plato, courage was deeply connected with the *emotions* and *knowledge,* and with operating according to the *right education.*

According to Socrates, all virtue was based on knowledge; the unexamined life was not worth living. In his conversations with Crito, Socrates said that: 'Your choice should be that of a good and courageous man—especially since you say you've had a lifelong concern for virtue.'

For Socrates, courage was founded on an understanding that:

Whether the multitude agrees or not, whether we must suffer things still worse than this or things more easy to bear, still the doing of injustice is in every circumstance shameful and evil for him who does it.

In other words, we should think of what one man, who understands things just and unjust, and understands the very truth itself, would say about our actions. For Socrates, courage depended on a sense of justice, and justice is the sum of all of the individual virtues. These virtues connected the external world of action with the internal world of knowledge.

Aristotle believed that courage, or fortitude, is the 'intermediate' between the defect of cowardice and the excess of rashness. Put another way, we can think of courage as flanked by two alternatives—its opposite, the cowering timidity that dares not act; and its counterfeit, the bravura and foolhardiness that looks a bit like courage but isn't. The courage that is truly moral, then, has a *moderating restraint* built into it. For Aristotle, courage arose when a good person controlled a genuine and realistically-based feeling of fear for the sake of a noble reason. In other words, *courage stops a correct action being hampered by fear.* It is as much about avoiding rashness as it is about overcoming fear. Ignorance of danger, pain or fear is not courageous—courage requires conscious, intellectual action.

Leadership and courage

In political leadership, courage is *setting a direction for the long term and taking people with you.* Many view the style of today's political leaders as cautious, not prepared to get ahead of the pack or to initiate reform. At times, our political leaders appear unprepared to truly lead in a bold, audacious manner and seem to look in the rear vision mirror in order to decide where to go next.

In the television series, *Yes Minister,* the senior public servant, Humphrey Appleby, would attempt to dissuade the Minister from proceeding with a particular action by saying: 'Oh, yes Minister, that would be terribly courageous!' In the political arena, Humphrey equated courage with rashness.

Former Prime Minister, Paul Keating, singled out two key elements of leadership—*imagination* and *courage.* Keating said:

Between the conception and the execution, there is faith, hope and courage. Leaders fail when they imagine things but don't do them. We have to be bold and faithful to ourselves.

Paul Keating's Press Secretary, Don Watson, in his recent memoir, *Recollections of a Bleeding Heart,* emphasised the importance of courage in Keating's leadership style:

Courage was Keating's hallmark and his stock in trade, as for some politicians it is nous, charm or practicality. Keating had these other attributes but it did not define him in a way that courage did. Courage was a prime element in the Keating mythos and a sign of weakness or a failure of will was a sign that the game was over.

This is echoed by the grand old man of US economics, John Kenneth Galbraith:

All the great leaders have had one characteristic in common: it was the willingness to confront unequivocally the major anxiety of their people in their time. This is the essence of leadership.

John Kotter says that leadership is primarily about *change* and *action*. The prerequisite for these is courage—courage to develop a different vision and strategy, to empower others to act, to have the strength of character to set the right examples and to persist despite the pain and sacrifices involved in change.

Change is an imperative for any organisation, but it takes courage to tackle the very real risks associated with it. Yet, as Charles Darwin once said, 'it is not the strongest that survive, nor the most intelligent, but the ones most responsive to change'.

The plains of Siberia are littered with the bones of sled drivers who thought that they would rest up for the night and that the pursuing wolves would do the same.   Anon

If leadership is about change, then one of the main roles of the leader is to reduce uncertainty and fear; fear of failure, fear of change and fear of voicing an opinion. These fears are the enemies of timely action, responsiveness, flexibility and commitment, and the subsequent waste they cause is enormous. In a change situation, until fear is at least minimised, there will be information hoarding instead of sharing, delaying tactics will be the norm, indecisiveness or 'safe' decisions will prevail, and politics will be the hallmark throughout the organisation. The leader must demonstrate courage, and engender courage in others by encouraging them to face and overcome their fears.

As with political leadership, courage in business leadership is about adopting a vision and strategy and taking your people with you on a journey that involves fundamental change.

Self-awareness

Just as courage is an essential element of effective leadership, *self-awareness* is one of the most important ingredients of courage.

Neither courage nor leadership can be founded on the actions of an individual who lacks self-awareness. Such actions are closer to rashness than courage. So courage in leaders (whether it be in the context of business, politics or anything else) is underpinned by *unsparing self-examination.*

Psychologist and author, Daniel Goleman, has found that effective leaders have a high degree of emotional intelligence: 'Without it, a person can have the best training in the world, an incisive, analytical mind and an endless supply of smart ideas, but he still won't make a great leader.'

Emotional intelligence distinguishes outstanding leaders (and can also be linked to strong performance). The first component of emotional intelligence is self-awareness, that is, a deep understanding of our emotions, strengths, weaknesses, needs and drives. People with strong self-awareness assess themselves and others with honesty. *They understand their own values* and the effect they have on others.

Thousands of years ago, the Greek oracle from Delphi gave the advice: Know thyself. Today, most leadership analysts regard this as the first commandment of leadership. As Goleman says: 'The decisions of self-aware people mesh with their values. A person who lacks self-awareness is apt to make decisions that bring on inner turmoil by treading on buried values.'

So, a key component of courage is self-awareness and a realistic assessment of yourself and of the moral framework that you believe should guide your actions. In the words of author Bill Newman:

Courage means that you will do what you believe to be right, regardless of the consequences.

Moral courage and integrity

Another key ingredient of leadership is *integrity.* Leadership integrity is grounded in *knowing what's right and then acting on it* (or conversely, not acting on what you know to be wrong). But it takes courage to lead and act with integrity—moral courage.

The effective leader has a self-belief and clear set of values that are grounded in a strong personal ethical framework. Ideally, the organisation will also have a clearly articulated vision, mission and values, against which every decision can be measured. But what happens when you work for a company that does not espouse your values? Or when you are required to take action that is consistent with the company's values but conflicts with your own? The result is a serious test of moral courage.

The foundation of integrity and ethical behaviour is conscience, but there are two forms of conscience. The first is the inner voice that knows what's right and what's not—this is the basis of a person's individual values. The second form of conscience is the inner voice that warns us that someone may be looking—the fear of being caught. Fear is hardly a strong philosophical base for a self-imposed code of commercial behaviour. Sadly, it seems that in many instances individuals have to be faced with risk (either personal, legal or financial) before they will do the right thing and take an ethical stance—which leads to speculation about how much supposedly ethical behaviour in business is actually a result of 'cold feet'!

Moral courage plays itself out daily in our lives. According to the Institute for Global Ethics:

Without moral courage, our brightest virtues rust from lack of use and with it we, at times, reap unexpected successes.

Moral courage is about facing mental challenges that are deeply connected with our core moral values. It is the positive courage to be *ethical in the face of a conscious awareness of the risks*.

A classic example of moral courage is the 'whistle-blower', someone who reports fraud and corruption in his or her place of employment. In the process these people face the real possibility of ruining their careers, losing their friends and being regarded as traitors.

It is important to note the difference between moral courage and 'economic' courage. Economic courage involves facing risk to achieve financial gain. Though the two types of courage are not incompatible, and in fact both are needed for business success, an act of economic courage can be carried out at the expense of principles and ethical behaviour.

The recent high profile corporate collapses (Enron, WorldCom,

HIH, and so on) demonstrate the results of a lack of integrity by executives. Many executives acted with complete disregard for accepted values of honesty and integrity in the pursuit of corporate (and in many cases, personal) economic gain. With very few exceptions, they did not have the moral courage to uphold fundamental ethical standards and confront unacceptable behaviours and practices.

Moral courage in business is most commonly displayed in a *steadfast adherence to the fundamental views of justice, honesty and fairness*. The corporate failures just mentioned have highlighted how important this is. It is moral courage that rises to defend principles not property, virtues not valuables. Acts of moral courage carry with them risk of humiliation, ridicule, contempt, unemployment and loss of social standing. In encouraging ethical business behaviour, the key principle is the behaviour of the *individuals* within the organisation. It is easy enough to establish organisational principles for ethical business behaviour, but it is the individuals within the organisation that have to be persuaded to include those principles in their work.

Robert E Kelley cogently argues that those who are being led also need courage. As he says:

No follower operating in this bottom-line fixated business environment (with short-termism), and who will likely work for several organisations over the span of a career, can expect to breeze through the years without facing at least one crisis of conscience over a disagreement with the leader.

A number of the recent company failures have again confirmed how desperately important are morally courageous acts from followers in organisations.

Each enterprise needs a positive culture that encourages respect for interdependence without personal greed, and in which the ethics of real people can flourish. This is more than a moral imperative, it is what is necessary for business survival.

Rushworth M Kidder said that:

Moral courage creates better cultures in organisations. The moral climate of any organisation is created through the choices and behaviours of its members.

But the willingness to make those choices and practise those behaviours can hinge on a willingness to face up to difficult moral issues. In other words, to be morally courageous.

These are definitely stressful times for leaders in any field. What is required is *the courage to care*; to care enough about your deeply held personal principles to be able to hold to them, even when facing personal risk.

A failure of courage

The recent massive corporate failures in Australia, the USA and other Western countries not only represent, as *Business Week* says, 'corrupt and unethical behaviour on an unimaginable scale', but also major failures of courage.

John Kenneth Galbraith has examined what he sees as the failure of courage and the conspiracy of silence that allowed Enron and WorldCom to reel out of control. He draws parallels with the events recounted so memorably in his book, *The Great Crash: 1929*. He wrote of the financial luminaries of that era:

They remain very quiet. The sense of responsibility in the financial community for the community as a whole is not small. It is nearly nil. To speak out against madness may be to ruin those who have succumbed to it. So the wise on Wall Street are nearly always silent. The foolish have the field to themselves and no-one rebukes them.

Seventy years later, history is repeated. 'There's still a tradition, a culture of restraint that keeps one from attacking one's colleagues, one's co-workers, no matter how wrong they seem to be', Galbraith said in an interview with *The Globe and Mail Canada*. He further spoke of this failure of nerve and courage when he said: 'In any great organisation it is far, far safer to be wrong with the majority than to be right alone.'

Public trust in the basic truthfulness of companies or their corporate leaders is coming undone. People everywhere are asking: Who and what can you trust? According to the latest Gallup Poll, public confidence in big business is at its lowest level since 1981. And based on the structuring of executive compensation packages and the fact that turnover for chief executives has never been higher, it takes a certain courage these days for business leaders to look beyond this year's results to the long-term health of the organisation.

The old adage, 'you get the behaviours you reward' may never be more appropriate than in these times of 'corporate excess' and unethical behaviour on a massive scale. These acts of weakness by certain corporate leaders have, to a significant extent, been driven not only by poor corporate governance practices, but also by remuneration packages that have fostered short-term thinking, greed and a widespread suspension of acceptable values. Also by an absence of courage.

It is instructive to look at the recent issues surrounding the world's most prestigious consulting firm, McKinsey & Co. McKinsey worked closely on strategy and business models with Enron. It had an extensive involvement with that company at all levels and wielded influence throughout Enron.

McKinsey changed its practices to link its fee structure to client performance. Was this what led to them taking a short-term view of Enron and focusing on the wrong things? Questions are now being raised as to how McKinsey could not have known about the fraudulent accounting practices. Did it ignore warning flags in order to keep an important account that was worth US$10 million in annual fees? In other words, did it avoid the truth and/or suspend its disbelief to preserve a lucrative relationship? In the words of a former McKinsey consultant who worked at Enron: 'Could they have seen the organisation as malfunctioning and spoken up? The answer is yes.' Too many firms will avoid the truth in the interests of revenue growth.

The espoused core values of McKinsey should have resulted in McKinsey management rejecting the unethical and immoral behaviours of senior Enron executives. Instead, courage failed.

Case studies in courageous leadership

Businessmen are being attacked for poor leadership in the community. Greg Barns, the previous Chairman of the Republican Movement, bemoans the business community's lack of courage to criticise government decisions for fear of losing out on government largesse. There are, however, many examples of true courage in business leadership, involving such things as a dramatic change in corporate strategy, a major corporate acquisition and downsizing exercises. Their hallmark is that these examples were founded on the leader's *high levels of self-awareness and deeply held beliefs.*

Humility and resolve

Jim Collins, in his book *Good to Great*, describes how 'good' companies transformed themselves into 'great' companies. He examined companies that made the leap from good to great results and sustained them for at least 15 years. These companies achieved extraordinary results, averaging cumulative stock returns 6.9 times those of the general market in the 15 years beyond a transition point.

Collins was surprised to find that the leaders of 'great' companies had what he called 'a paradoxical blend of personal humility and professional will'. They had a ferocious resolve and maintained an unwavering faith that they could and would prevail in the end. An example of this type of leadership courage was Darwin E Smith of Kimberley-Clark.

Darwin Smith was commonly perceived as a humble man (and in his younger years, perhaps for very good reasons). In his role as CEO, however, this reserved man blended personal humility and fierce resolve with solid self-awareness and his core values of integrity and honesty. With these attributes he demonstrated the most remarkable courage in completely changing corporate strategy and transforming his company in the process.

When Smith was appointed CEO of Kimberley-Clark, he turned a 'stodgy old paper company' into the leading paper-based consumer products company in the world. Shortly after becoming CEO, he made the most remarkable decision in the company's history—to sell the paper mills. He formed the view that the traditional core business could only generate mediocre returns in the future. Smith was betting the company's and his own future on an aggressive move from a commercial arena of weak competition into an area of intense world-class competition; the consumer paper products industry. It was a case of 'achieve greatness or perish'.

Smith's decision to sell the mills and invest all the funds in the consumer business was regarded by one board member as the most courageous move he's ever seen a CEO make. As Collins said, it was 'like the General who burned the boats upon landing, leaving only one option (succeed or die)'. The business media labelled the move 'dumb' and industry analysts downgraded the stock, but 25 years later the company beat all industry performance benchmarks and its leading competitor in most product categories.

This was the story of an extremely humble man with strong values and self-belief taking the most courageous business decisions.

Composure under pressure

In a recent *Harvard Business Review* article, leadership experts highlighted the importance of leaders demonstrating personal courage by *maintaining composure under pressure*—being unflappable.

The CEO of Merck Pharmaceuticals, Raymond Gilmartin, tells the story:

For the good of the organisation you can't let them throw you. I was in my office one day and someone came in with unexpected news that could have a significant impact on the company. In the face of news like that, you have to be unflappable.

You have to show that you understand completely the seriousness of the situation. It's very important to the organisation that you face these situations with some sort of personal courage. If I had panicked, if I had said how could you have let this happen, everyone would have frozen.

Frederick Smith, CEO of FedEx in the USA, echoed these sentiments in an interview:

What you call being unflappable sounds more like courage to me. Leaders have to be capable of dealing with problems and issues that demand a fair bit of courage. I mean I can be totally unflappable and be absolutely stupid. But seeing a threat coming down and staying calm, now that's a different matter. Your organisation needs to see you maintain your calm but that has to be accompanied by a lot of activity. You have to be decisive, set clear directions and keep moving.

You have to show you're not immobilised by a crisis.

So, composure under significant business pressure is another essential ingredient of leadership that is founded in courage.

Vulnerability

A business leader also displays courage by making herself *vulnerable* and accessible to employees. Some people label this 'soft' management. But soft management doesn't necessarily equate to 'weak' management. It also can be a show of strength and courage.

Consider the case of William Peace (as reported in the *Harvard Business Review*). Against the advice of his people he met alone with some employees that he had just laid off. At the time, Peace was head of the Synthetic Fuels Division of Westinghouse. With a decline in oil prices, Westinghouse's top management had decided to sell the division within a few months or face liquidation. There were very few buyers and for the division's employees, closure would mean the end of building a great business. To make the division a more attractive acquisition prospect it was necessary to lay off 15 people.

In the past, when people were chosen to be laid off, the individual managers would break the bad news to them. But William Peace would have none of that. Against the admonitions of his managers, he met with the 15 employees on the force-in-reduction list to give his personal reasons for the lay-offs. Peace knew that this was the moral thing to do, but he also hoped that this action would give the survivors in the division more trust and confidence in the division's future and the security of their own positions.

In the meeting, Peace asked them not to blame their managers or themselves and explained that the decision was in no way 'a value judgement on them as individuals'. He said to them that if they wanted someone to blame, then blame him. He explained the commercial imperatives behind the decision.

Peace gained a sense that the workers understood the reasons for the lay-offs and even respected what the company was trying to do. For the surviving employees, there was a renewed determination to hold the business together, even if it would mean a change of owners. The meeting was a success, not only because the employees understood the key messages—that executives would do everything to keep the business alive and lay-offs were a last resort—but also, and primarily, because Peace made himself vulnerable to the criticism, disapproval and anger of the people he was laying off.

It took courage for Peace to confront the anger in the way he did. It was an emotionally bruising encounter, but *his courage was underpinned by his core set of values*. These included openness, integrity and a belief that people should be treated with dignity.

Holding steady

In the Australian corporate scene, there have been many examples of courage. Chris Corrigan of Patrick Corporation demonstrated the courage of his convictions, based on strong self-belief and solid values, in his efforts to transform the values and practices of the company's waterfront workers in 2000.

Chris Corrigan knew the risk of taking on the entrenched practices of this industry. His life, and the lives of his family, were threatened. But he understood the imperatives for change and had the deep set of personal beliefs and the inner strength to see it through.

As Ronald Heifetz said in *The Work of Leadership*: 'Leadership demands a deep understanding of the pain of change—the fears and sacrifices associated with major readjustment—it also requires the ability to hold steady and maintain the tension.' Chris Corrigan demonstrated the most fundamental understanding of this.

Robert Champion de Crespigny, the Chief Executive of Normandy Mining, clearly demonstrated courageous leadership in his stance on Aboriginal reconciliation in the mid-nineties. This stance was seen as being at odds with his commercial interests. He believed that there were clear moral and economic reasons why reconciliation was important. Morally, it is a question of social justice and economically, it brings longer lasting commercial outcomes. Robert Champion de Crespigny courageously demonstrated that moral and economic considerations are inextricably linked.

Commitment to vision

Andrew Carnegie was one of the giants of US industry and, as described by Richard S Tedlow in the article 'What titans can tell us', was responsible for a technological breakthrough that opened up the possibility of producing steel in undreamed-of quantities. Carnegie was convinced that steel would change the material basis of civilisation in the last quarter of the nineteenth century.

Carnegie is regarded as a titan because he had *the courage to bet on his vision* of market potential and create an industry. He was not constrained by history and refused to be frightened by precedent. He had neither compunction nor hesitation about 'breaking the eggs that went into his omelette'.

Like other titans (Henry Ford, Thomas J Watson, Sam Walton) Carnegie was incapable of being discouraged. He didn't look back. Whatever problem he had faced in the past, he was not afraid of the future, because he planned to play a big role in creating it. Also like other business leaders of courage, he didn't let an all-encompassing focus on the success of his business undermine his personal values and he didn't blame others for his problems.

As Tedlow says, there are a number of themes that recur in the conduct of business titans. A clear mission and consistent messages were keys to making their dreams a reality. So was an *unflinching commitment to the fulfilment of their destinies*. Carnegie's certainty in the face of an uncertain world was a beacon for attracting and motivating followers. We can take inspiration and ideas from this courageous giant of enterprise.

Alignment of commercial and personal values

It is difficult at times to separate moral courage from good business nous. For example, was it courage and adherence to ethical standards or simply good commercial sense for Tylenol (in the USA in the eighties, and more recently Herron Pharmaceuticals in Australia) to respond to a product tampering scare in one small region by withdrawing all its products from shelves in all retail outlets throughout the USA?

Tylenol expressed its deep concerns for the potential risks to customers and acted immediately. It could have down-played the issue, waited for further evidence of the problem and argued against the risks. This would have been an easier step. But by taking the bold and courageous step of completely withdrawing its products, Tylenol engendered a trust and confidence that translated to an increase in market share when Tylenol tamper-proof products were finally returned to the retailers' shelves.

Contrast this with Perrier and the public's concern with certain chemicals discovered in its bottled waters. It took the less audacious approach, publicly trivialising its product contamination issue and refusing to withdraw its products when the public perceived a product health risk. The company suffered the inevitable commercial consequences.

An example of a leader successfully aligning commercial imperatives with personal values involved the former Chief Executive of British Airways, Colin Marshall. In the eighties, Marshall determined that, in order to meet the challenges of new markets, his organisation needed to learn to adapt quickly to changing conditions. He identified a strong business case for transforming his airline into an 'exemplar of customer service', but at the same time he also wished to align the organisation with his own deeply held (but quite different) values.

It was Marshall's belief that his organisation must become dedicated not only to serving people but also to acting on trust, respecting the individual and making teamwork happen across boundaries. People had to learn to collaborate and develop a collective sense of responsibility for outcomes. The blame mentality that was a key feature of British Airways had to be eradicated. He was one of the first executives to make 'creating trust' a priority.

This courageous change of strategy and transformation effort, which enabled British Airways to rise to new market challenges, was founded on the CEO and his leadership team understanding themselves and having the emotional strength to tolerate the uncertainty and the frustration.

Marshall demonstrated that courage in leadership is a function of self-awareness, strong values and solid resolve, and that it is particularly dependent on taking personal responsibility for decisions and outcomes.

Change of direction

Fundamental changes in vision and strategy, and the transformation efforts that must be undertaken to achieve the changes, require courageous leadership.

Lou Gerstner had the courage to adapt, change and transform his business to ensure its ongoing survival. He became president of the Travel Related Services (TRS) arm of American Express (Amex) in the eighties. At that time, Gerstner faced one of the biggest challenges in Amex's 130-year history—the onslaught of hundreds of banks offering credit cards and financial services, and other firms offering traveller's cheques.

In response, Gerstner challenged and changed the very notion of the company's business, thereby totally transforming it. He segmented the market and developed a range of innovative products and services. He invested in productivity, introduced dramatic changes in the culture of the organisation and rewarded risk-taking. This courageous transformation effort paid off. TRS's net income increased by a compounded annual rate of around 18 per cent and return on equity reached 28 per cent.

Staying focused

It takes courage to say no to certain business, particularly when your company is in an early growth phase. Many companies are interested in growth for growth's sake—no matter what business is attracted.

This type of courage requires a clear knowledge of your business model, your mission and values, and the clients or customers that are right for your business—and then adhering to this model. This may mean making tough decisions about the clients you are prepared to work with and those you are not, as well as the employees you believe should be working for you and those who should not. In an early growth phase for a company, this unswerving focus will take some courage.

For one US executive search firm, saying yes to the wrong business created margin pressures and employee morale issues, and damaged its reputation as servicing standards slipped. Susan Bishop, the CEO of Bishop Partners, found it was difficult to maintain the essential discipline of saying no to the wrong kind of business—business that did not fit the company's business model and corporate values. Saying no consistently is hard and requires a certain level of courage when business results are below expectations. The wrong business drained a disproportionate amount of time and effort for this firm and, as Susan Bishop said, 'prevented it from taking on more promising work that appeared halfway through the job'.

The experience of Bishop Partners is that you must realistically define your core business, have the courage to change the business model if the marketplace changes, but also have the *courage to remain focused* and say no to business that doesn't fit your business model description.

A personal story

In the past, in my chief executive officer roles, there have been a few occasions when I have had to make redundant many employees because of uncompetitive cost structures. If we had not acted to place ourselves in cost-competitive positions, these companies would have been slowly liquidated.

Some would say that a CEO's role is wonderful moments strung together between hours of terror! Well, I quickly came to understand the meaning of this soon after I was appointed CEO of one particular company. The ground rules had changed, our competitive position had shifted overnight and we needed to move quickly to hold our previously unchallenged leadership position. We quickly realised what Tom Peters had meant when he'd said: 'Today's laurels are tomorrow's compost.'

The overnight and radical shift by our competitor to a greenfield, non-unionised and very modern site meant that they were set to be 50 per cent more productive than we would be. We couldn't let that happen. The demand that we make rapid change was itself an opportunity—but we needed to make sure the change was right, and big and fast enough. We needed modern work practices that would drive costs down and we needed to concentrate on the core business activity.

An inevitable outcome of meeting these objectives was a reduction in staff across the whole business, halving the number of levels in the management structure and redesigning almost every job in the company. This significant change program reduced our operations people by 40 per cent. The nature of the change and the manner in which it was carried out, whilst commercially defensible, had a severe impact on trust and confidence in the company.

As CEO, I held a strong belief that the workforce should be treated with respect, honesty and openness, dignity and worth. The actions we were taking were certainly economically courageous, but I knew that if I was to begin to restore an acceptable level of trust and confidence in the company, then I would need to personally brief all employees as to why the decisions were taken and what the company objectives were from this point.

I briefed groups of 10–50 team members. At times it was heart rending, because I could see the impact on them of losing their work buddies and the damage to their belief in their future with the company.

In one briefing session, I spoke to a group of night shift employees at around midnight, outlining the inevitability of the changes and the company's objectives. After 20 minutes, I asked for questions and responses. No-one spoke. You could feel the tension in the room. I said: 'Look, I'm not leaving here until you ask me questions and you let me know your views.' And, boy, did they unleash it! All the hostility came out about the trust that they felt had been abused as a result of this tough change program. For the next half hour they vented their anger, but they also listened to my reasoning as to why these changes could not have been avoided if we were to remain a viable entity.

Now, I don't believe that I necessarily changed their views about me and my management team, but I do believe that at least they respected me for giving them the opportunity to focus on the person that they saw as being responsible for these tough decisions. Also, like William Peace at Westinghouse, by giving them the freedom to complain, argue, even to attack me, I made myself vulnerable to these people. Because I avoided defensiveness and opened myself up to criticism, they were much more inclined to believe that the strength and force of my position was not merely contrived and rhetorical, but was real.

By holding to my values and arguing my actions, I believe that I gained more credibility. By demonstrating my core values of honesty, openness and integrity, I was taking one of the early steps in the process of restoring an acceptable level of trust in the company and me. I could have avoided delivering the messages myself and avoided the face to face consequences of delivering bad news, but in my view this would have been weak and poor leadership.

It takes courage for any business leader to be open-minded and responsible enough to walk straight into adversity rather than seeking to avoid it. But *the very essence of leadership is having the courage of your convictions.* At times, by sharing a willingness to confront unpopular decisions and by being vulnerable to emotional crossfire, you do stand as Lee Iacocca once said, on a 'precipice of indignity and lost authority'. In the end you must show the sensitivity and candour that is essential to your leadership position.

In this company, we created small, autonomous working teams, flattened management layers, introduced flexibilities and customer service focus. We grew new communications channels and we saw greater recognition of our genuine commitment to openness, trust and flexibility.

The changed structure opened up development opportunities for our people, it broke down barriers and generated shifts in the culture with better-based values. There were fewer road blocks for people and enhanced responsibilities.

All these changes were founded on an economically courageous shift in strategy coupled with morally courageous actions taken by a number of leaders throughout the organisation.

Against the odds

Finally, how about this fine and stirring example of a truly courageous man who struggled against the odds. Bill Newman describes it in *The 10 Laws of Leadership Vision*:

He drifted through his twenties. When he turned 31, he thought, 'I've got to get myself going and do something!' He formed a partnership and went into business, but in 18 months he was bankrupt. Then he decided, since he was broke anyway, he would go into politics. In his first local election he lost badly. Two years later, aged 34, he went back into business. Bankruptcy again. A year later he thought things were improving when he fell in love with a beautiful woman. She died. At 36 he suffered a nervous breakdown and was confined to bed for six months. He recovered and went back into politics, running for another local government post. He lost again. He started another business, with a little more success this time. So at 43, he decided to run for Congress. He lost.

At 46, he ran for Congress again and he lost again. At 48 he ran for the Senate and lost that as well. When he was 55, he tried for his party's nomination for Vice President. He was badly defeated. At age 58, he ran for the Senate again, and again he lost. Finally, at 60 years of age, Abraham Lincoln was elected to his first office—President of the United States. Lincoln told his friends late in life that he had a lifelong battle with fear and depression but he wouldn't quit. Lincoln was a fighter, a man of courage, a winner.

Courageous governance

Recently there has been a lot of discussion about current board practices and the performance of boards and individual company directors. The pressure is on directors from all quarters, but in particular from an aggressively vigilant media. Boards of companies now face the real risk of public exposure if they fail to reach performance expectations, or they overpay directors and senior executives by failing to effectively link performance with rewards. Also if they fail to address conflict of interest and transparency issues.

There are a number of attributes that make for an effective director—imagination, integrity, intellectual capacity, technical skills and an intimate understanding of the business are just some. A key attribute, however, is courage.

Relationships within the board of directors should not become so close that directors place friendship, respect for others, or fear of causing offence above their primary responsibilities of steering the organisation's profitability and long-term viability. Nick Greiner, the former Premier of New South Wales and now professional company director, has said that too often questions are not asked or directors do not pursue information because mateship reigns and no-one wants to rock the boat. As he says, 'it is a collegial thing and it's a bit hard to buck that trend and ask a difficult question'.

On some boards, directors critique the performance of board members at the end of each board meeting. For many directors, this would be just too much. Too many directors do not have the needed inner strengths; they are laced with sensitivities. At times, we seem to be more concerned about accommodating the personal frailties of board members than about advancing the company's interests with best practices in the boardroom.

The testimony of HIH Insurance Chief Executive, Ray Williams, to the HIH Royal Commission is instructive. He questioned the courage of the HIH board in making an application to appoint a provisional liquidator and not attempting to trade out of HIH's 'economic difficulties'. Whether this is right or not, a lack of courage exhibited by individual HIH directors may also be reflected by an apparent lack of tension and conflict in the boardroom. Indeed, Ray Williams has testified that the HIH board meetings were 'very harmonious'.

The media magnate and arch rival of Rupert Murdoch, Robert Maxwell, brought into stark relief the lack of moral courage exhibited by the directors of his various group companies. As the owner of the Mirror Group in the UK and the publishers Macmillan in the USA, Maxwell was found by the UK corporate regulator to be unfit to run a public company. To paraphrase Oscar Wilde, he set low personal standards and then consistently failed to achieve them. Maxwell could very easily be defined by a statement that has been attributed to another of his ilk, who shall remain anonymous:

You're an intelligent person of great moral character who has taken a very courageous stand. I'm an intelligent person with no moral character at all; so I'm in an ideal position to appreciate it!

When his company was in trouble, Maxwell engaged in a range of unethical and/or illegal commercial practices, including the raiding of pension funds. He contained his critics both inside and outside his various companies through his forceful personality, threats of legal action or simply by rewarding directors or executives with remuneration levels that were well above market rates. Many of these individuals would have justified their unquestioning stances by agreeing with Woody Allen's statement: 'I'm not a coward, just the ultimate pragmatist!'

The deeply concerning issue is that Maxwell was able to undertake these repellent practices by leveraging human weaknesses and vanities, and in doing so he smothered the independent judgment of all except the strongest individuals. His life demonstrated for some, as his biographer said, the 'paucity of independent spirits in our midst'.

A close associate of mine demonstrated a clear act of moral courage a few years ago when he 'blew the whistle' on a public accounting firm that had failed to adequately disclose to shareholders a fraud perpetrated by the managing director of a major public company. He publicly disclosed the fraud that triggered the sacking of the managing director and then promptly resigned from the accounting practice. His moral courage was founded on a breach of the values that he held sacred.

Conclusion

A successful leader in any arena, whether it is in politics or business, must have a number of attributes. These include integrity, openness and great communication skills. But, importantly, a successful leader today must have a capacity to realistically assess himself or herself and understand the personal values that truly matter in corporate behaviours. Self-awareness and deeply held beliefs are essential elements of courage; the very essence of leadership. Courageous acts are taken by self-aware people with fully meshed values.

Courage in business leadership is expressed in many ways. It can be changing a vision and strategy. It can be maintaining an ethical stance in the face of personal risks. Courage can be a key factor in driving out the fear that is prevalent in many companies. It can be about holding to a strategic choice and transformation efforts in the face of severe questioning from industry analysts and others. As a business leader, courage can involve confronting employees directly affected by your downsizing decisions and making yourself vulnerable to their criticisms and anger.

Leadership is about change and it takes real courage to maintain your resolve when the real risks of change become blindingly apparent. Courage is caring enough about your values that you uphold these in the face of risks.

While courage in leadership depends on self-aware people who understand their individual values, of equal importance is a clear and well established understanding throughout an organisation of its culture; its values. A well expressed code of conduct needs to permeate all organisational behaviours and language. The behaviours that it finds unacceptable need to be well understood. The company needs then to have the courage in its leadership to adhere to these beliefs in all corporate behaviours when another path may deliver greater short-term benefits. Effective corporate leadership occurs when moral courage and good business sense meet.

But the truly great leaders are the ones who are prepared to change and take a different path by developing a new vision and strategy that involve calculated risks.

The great leaders have the courage to fail and, from that failing, the courage to learn.

Seven key attributes of courage in leadership

1 Self-awareness with inner strength.
2 Deeply held personal values that include integrity, trust and openness.
3 Conscious awareness of the personal risks.
4 Strength of purpose with firmness of spirit.
5 Responsiveness to change.
6 A sense of justice.
7 Disciplined, ethical behaviour.

For further exploration

—D Goleman, *Emotional Intelligence*, Little, Brown, London, 1997. This is an interesting and constantly challenging exposition of the importance of emotional intelligence for effective leadership. It proves that emotional intelligence matters more than IQ.

—Jim Collins, *Good to Great*, Harper Business, New York, 2001. With superb research, Jim Collins and his team explain how a good company can become a great company and why some companies make the leap and others do not.

—*Harvard Business Review on What Makes a Leader*, Harvard Business School Press, Boston, 2001.

This is an excellent series of articles from the *Harvard Business Review* on the leadership characteristics that work. This series explores the question 'Why should anyone be led by you?' and represents the latest thinking in the field of leadership. Includes *HBR* articles from Daniel Goleman and Michael Maccoby.

INTEGRITY   **3**

Margaret Thorsborne

About the author

Margaret Thorsborne, BSc, Dip Ed, Grad Dip Counselling, FAIM

Margaret Thorsborne is the Managing Director of Transformative Justice Australia (Queensland). She assists public and private sector organisations to manage and overcome problems with workplace relationships, particularly workplace bullying, sexual harassment, misconduct, inappropriate behaviour, diminished work performance, aggressive management and supervision, dysfunctional teams and high level conflict.

She began her professional career as a high school teacher before becoming a school counsellor and then an internal consultant and project manager for the Queensland Education Department, specialising in the fields of behaviour, trauma and conflict management. Today she is internationally recognised as an expert on school and workplace bullying and restorative behaviour management practices. She bases her work in a range of disciplines including biology, psychology, criminal justice, political philosophy, and social, organisational and management theory.

Margaret has presented papers, seminars and workshops and conducted training throughout Australia, New Zealand, Canada, the UK and the USA. She has had papers published on restorative justice as it applies to schools and workplaces, and on recruitment and selection based on workplace literacy and numeracy skills. She is currently the chair of the board of an international non-profit community sector organisation based in Queensland, and is a member of the Australian Institute of Management Sunshine Coast Regional Committee.

Margaret Thorsborne can be reached at marg@thorsborne.com.au or www.thorsborne.com.au.

Introduction

I sit in the second pew from the front at the funeral of Bill Brown, my father-in-law, holding hands with my sons and listening to my husband struggling to stay composed as he speaks about the sort of father Bill had been. My husband's siblings and their wives, husbands and children are here too, mourning the loss of a much-loved 86-year-old who had died after a long spell in a nursing home.

I glance back and, through my tears, see a large number of men, all looking a bit more grizzled and stooped than the last time I saw them. I finally realise that these are the men who worked with and for Bill in his time as a senior public servant. One of them comes forward to speak of Bill's work life.

Bill's passing and funeral did not make the papers. He was not a public figure—he was what is known as a quiet achiever. But the story told that morning about his vision for his work, his values, intelligence, commitment, grace, humour, compassion, humility, the way he led, his influence in his field and the legacy it left, was testament to the worthiness of his life. His children were right to be so proud. He was, indeed, a man of integrity.

Writing this chapter has been an interesting journey. Frankly, I was seduced by Robyn, the editor, into taking up the challenge— a moment of weakness! It coincided with a trip to the UK for work, and while I was there and then on my exhausted return the job loomed over me like a black cloud. I would gladly have found someone to pass the baton to. But in the end, how could I let someone down having made such a commitment? What would that say about my own integrity? So here I am, in the dawn hours of each morning between here and the deadline, with my cat for company and my family asleep upstairs. Actually quite enjoying myself in the moment.

So, where to start? I began by nailing every intelligent person I know with this question: 'Think of a boss, manager, leader or someone in your life who you think has integrity. What does that mean to you?'

Phone calls, emails, talk lists, discussions over coffee, long and well-lubricated-with-a-fine-red chats at dinner and family gatherings. These folk loved talking about integrity. It was obviously an important issue. Naturally, I also read whatever I could, but that was a less enlightening experience than listening to people's real-world stories.

One thing stood out. Each person could only name a handful of people who they believed had the goods. But they could remember plenty of instances where integrity was absent and spoke of the resultant damage to themselves, others and the organisation.

It seems that integrity has become an old-fashioned virtue.

What is integrity?

The people I asked about integrity included CEOs, the middle and senior managers and staff of organisations of all sizes from the private and public sectors, consultants working in the field of organisational development, neighbours, close friends and family. When I asked whom they knew who had integrity I was saddened, but not surprised, at how few leaders, managers or bosses could be named. I can only name two in my own working life—more about them later.

These are the words that my respondents used when asked to describe the people they identified as possessing 'integrity':
— strength of character
— steadfast, resolute, having fibre
— walking the talk, doing what was promised
— authentic, straightforward, what's on the inside is displayed on the outside
— open, honest and direct in their dealings with others
— clear and uncompromised values, and clarity about what's right and wrong
— committed, with the courage of their convictions
— behaviours matched values (congruence)
— principled, honourable, fair, accountable and responsible
— balanced, integrated, whole
— self aware and self-reflective
— mature and wise.

And there was congruence between these responses and the various dictionary definitions that I gathered:

Integrity: *Steadfast adherence to a strict moral or ethical code. Moral soundness. Honesty. Freedom from corrupting influence or motive—used especially with reference to the fulfilment of contracts, the discharge of agencies, trusts and the like. Uprightness, rectitude. The quality or condition of being whole or undivided. Completeness.*

For good measure I also included 'integral' and 'integration' in my search for meaning:

Integral: *Essential or necessary for completeness; a whole; complete; perfect; uninjured; entire.*
Integration: *The organisation of the psychology or social traits and tendencies of a personality into a harmonious whole.*

Members of my informal focus group discussed and debated whether infamous leaders of recent times, such as Hitler, David Koresh and Osama bin Laden, could be said to have had integrity. They and others like them certainly adhere to a set of values that are clear and well communicated. They also have a clear sense of purpose and the capacity to inspire and lead. I suspect, however, that their influence over others was largely based on fear—and that doesn't count for integrity in my books.

So, for the purposes of this chapter, I will focus on a discussion of integrity and what most of us commonly understand as leadership *for good* rather than *for evil*; that is, where there is no intent to harm.

When integrity is absent

Newspapers are full of stories of people who demonstrate little integrity in their dealings with others, and how they damage others' wellbeing and livelihoods. I'll not bore you with more stories about Quintex, HIH, Enron, WorldCom or One.Tel, except to say that board members in those companies were obviously asleep at the wheel, and those who benefited, at least in the short term, subscribed to the 'greed is good' principle.

In general, politicians, intent on remaining in power or staying endorsed, vote along party or factional lines in matters of policy, unless they are permitted a conscience vote. Politics is a game of quid pro quo. It is a rare politician who is *seen* to have integrity.

Decisions are made on what voters will likely support. Staying in power is the highest priority. Integrity appears not to count. In my own state of Queensland, one exception stands out. Peter Wellington is the Independent MP for Nicklin. He was injured terribly in a tractor accident on his property, but turned up in a wheelchair for parliamentary sittings—long before his doctors recommended he return to work. His commitment to his electorate, and his steadfast principles about what he will and will not negotiate on, have earned him the respect of his colleagues, although it is fair to say that he has probably driven the ruling Labor government nuts in the process!

Apart from individuals, there are also industries that are perceived to lack integrity. Again I referred this issue to my informal focus group and they were quick to answer! The list of industries that people felt could not be trusted included real estate, retail car sales (in fact, sales in general), horse racing, banking, law and mortgage broking. Their responses were based on times when they felt they had been ripped off, or their interests as customers or consumers had been given low priority compared to the high priority of making a profit. (I'm very aware, however, that there are people who work in these industries who *do* have integrity, who *are* honest, put customer needs high on their lists and walk their talk. I also know that these people and their particular businesses reap the benefit with return custom and solid reputations for reliability. It would seem that integrity and profit do not need to be mutually exclusive.)

Law enforcement agencies form another group that suffers from a public perception of lack of integrity—often with good reason. Recently I listened to the Queensland Commissioner of Police discussing progress since the Fitzgerald inquiry into police corruption. Highly educated and widely travelled, he said that law enforcement typically moves through predictable phases of corruption and reform, followed by a period of *slippage.* He was intent on reassuring the Queensland public that our police were not yet sliding back into the 'bad old ways'. Clearly it takes a great deal of hard work to maintain integrity.

The greatest fallout from a lack of integrity is the *loss of trust* in institutions, industries, management and individuals. In the vacuum created when trust is lost, suspicion and paranoia thrive. Is it any wonder that we have lost faith in our institutions, management, the business world and those who lead us, and have become distrusting and cynical about the ability of those in authority to give priority to our welfare and wellbeing? As I mentioned earlier, integrity is an old-fashioned virtue that has become a low priority somewhere in the quest for increasing profit, market share, votes and tenure.

Loss of trust

Trust is an incredibly precious commodity, and is always the first casualty when relationships in the workplace are damaged. Through my work as an organisational development consultant, particularly in workplaces beset with high levels of conflict, I am immersed on a daily basis in situations that are 'emotionally toxic'. Whether the precipitating crisis is a formal complaint made by one employee about another (or about their manager), workplace harassment, diminished performance or some other destructive set of circumstances (that is, people behaving badly), what is common is the deterioration of relationships and the decrease of trust in management.

Goleman, Boyatzis and McKee (you may be familiar with Goleman's work on emotional intelligence) conclude that transparency—an authentic openness to others about one's feelings, beliefs and actions—engenders integrity, or the sense that a leader can be trusted; that he (or she) lives by his values and is genuine. They also stress that integrity is a leadership virtue and an organisational strength.

Yet the *Australian Business Leadership Survey*—a recent study of Australian managers conducted by the Australian Institute of Management and Monash University, and involving self-assessment of leadership skills, organisational culture and job outcomes—stated that:

Managers by and large don't feel their staff trust them. One conclusion that can be drawn from this finding is that managers have failed to recognise the strategic advantage of instilling a culture of trust within their organisation.

In recent years, my approach to solving workplace problems has been grounded in the field of *restorative justice*. Restorative justice is a process of transacting justice that is transforming the world of criminal justice in Western democracies. It embodies a philosophy and practice of problem solving that views misconduct and crime as a violation of people and relationships. These violations create obligations and liabilities. The solution lies in repairing the harm; making amends. The priority is healing, not retribution. I believe that this philosophy can be applied just as effectively in the realm of organisational management and leadership, and for facilitating justice within workplaces.

Through my practice, I have come to understand that we cannot afford to ignore the emotional fallout from inappropriate behaviour and/or poor management practices and policies. People get hurt. When it becomes chronic, it is an enormous distraction and makes people sick. They become demotivated. Job satisfaction and productivity suffer. There are significant economic costs to the organisation. I see chronic shame and chronic distress everywhere (more about shame later). Without exception, there is a loss of trust and, nearly always, integrity is missing.

On the rare occasions that integrity is present in these toxic situations, it is usually shown by an isolated individual who struggles to stay resolute in the face of very difficult circumstances. Sadly, this person is often *not* the manager or CEO. Maintaining integrity in a workplace where there is incredible pressure to cave in, roll over or give up takes courage. Integrity is not easy to do.

Integrity in action

In my interventions in troubled workplaces, the healing process depends on individuals of integrity who can model appropriate behaviours and help lead the group out of trouble. Through their actions, they demonstrate to others that integrity is a worthy virtue. They help others to understand that honesty in dealing with each other, knowing the difference between right and wrong, having courage to do what is right, and caring about relationships can improve outcomes for individuals and for the organisation.

YOUR FIRST CHALLENGE:

Think about someone you know who has integrity.

— *Identify their values regarding work, productivity, matters of right and wrong, fairness and relationships.*

— *What do they say about their values?*

— *How do they enact these values and beliefs? In what ways do they walk their talk?*

In preparing to write the chapter, I surveyed my professional colleagues about their experiences of leadership with integrity. Here are some of their stories about leadership with integrity.

Bruce's story

From a colleague, Bruce, who works in health care in Philadelphia.

As a director of Mental Health practices (1999–2002) I supervised five different staffing groups for Outpatient Services. Always, the most glaring inequity in the businesses was that classism was an accepted value. By that I mean that the lower-wage people worked harder and had less independence, and clinical staff always violated the administrative staff boundaries. They not only expected to be able to give assignments to staff already responsible for every ringing phone and every live person in the office, but also had tantrums about any lapses in their needs being met.

For me as a leader, integrity means ensuring that classism is not practised in the office. I protect the people who have the most difficult jobs, and expect people with private offices and their own phones to operate independently and self-sufficiently (as I do, and did when in their positions).

Surprisingly, this is viewed as a very radical leadership value. Both clinical and administrative staff have clearly stated that this has never been suggested or employed in their previous workplaces.

Of course, some of the clinical staff feel cheated and confused, while the administrative staff feel protected, appreciated and understood for the value they bring to a functional environment. I just think of this as managing the team so that everyone is treated fairly, and that job duties are the only pressures that need to be tolerated at work.

Jackie's story

From a clinical psychologist, Jackie, also in health care, in
Washington, DC.

*I'm in my fifties, and I can only think of one manager in my entire
professional career who had integrity as an outstanding characteristic. Sad, isn't
it? He's the medical director of the department I work for at present. He is low-
key, caring and firm. He has always encouraged us to work as hard as we
possibly could, and consistently praised employees who went above and beyond.*

*The reason I say he has integrity is that he works harder than any of
us, often putting in 80-hour weeks. The really sad part about this is that
he has been diagnosed with leukaemia and now, for the first time in his
life, he is actively seeking a more balanced lifestyle.*

*The other manager of my department is a very warm woman—she
always smiles and says encouraging things, and tells you to take care of
yourself . . . and then never supports you when it comes down to the task
(and who, by the way, does not take care of herself). She constantly
stimulates interest–excitement, and then, just as constantly, induces shame.*

*I like her, but do not respect her, and certainly feel she shows a
complete lack of integrity.*

Sarah's story

This is a story of my own, about a woman that I know and
respect for her integrity.

*Sarah (not her real name) is a middle manager in a large public sector
organisation. She is one of the two people I can name who possess the
virtue of integrity in spades. Before her latest promotion, Sarah was the
organisational Workplace Health and Safety trouble-shooter, with a
particular interest in emotional health. She insisted that 'toxic' work units
were cleaned up, and damaged relationships healed.*

*Sarah takes great care of people who are suffering. Utterly reliable, she
is called on to fix things, and I am often contracted to provide the skills to
help her in this work. It is wonderful to work with Sarah. Her
commitment to the organisation and its goals is very high. Her
commitment to management and staff wellbeing is enormous—often to her
own personal cost, physically and emotionally.*

*Her increasingly high profile and popularity amongst senior executive
managers as reliable and trustworthy (she has saved their bacon on many an*

occasion) mean that she has been the subject of the 'tall poppy' syndrome. I suspect that by walking her talk, she has shamed other, less principled, colleagues in some way and so they have taken every opportunity to punish her. Snide comments, open hostility, formal complaints that she had interfered with their chances of promotion (by showing them up), a whisper in the ear of someone powerful—these all hurt her feelings badly.

Despite this, she would not deviate from her work of transforming soured workplace relationships. When things go wrong between her and someone in her team, she gives and invites honest feedback. She has done the painful work of self-reflection. She is a quietly committed Christian, and this obviously plays a significant role in her values.

Her leadership in the work she does has been exemplary. Working with her has been an absolute treat. Together, we have achieved some remarkable outcomes in work units that have been virtually totally dysfunctional. Personal integrity and integrity of process have paid off.

Sadly, recently, she has become the victim of a stalker; one of the many disturbed individuals she has assisted in the organisation. And, finally, the cost of her selfless devotion to the care of others has taken its toll and temporarily undone her. She has taken stress leave in an attempt to find relief from the daily fear she now experiences.

This woman has integrity. It is hard work and it has cost her. I wish I could bottle it to anoint others who are missing it. I feel better about myself when I am with her.

YOUR SECOND CHALLENGE

Ask yourself:

— *What's your talk? How do you walk it?*

— *What are the circumstances that see you keep silent in the face of violations of your values about work? What are the pressures on you in that moment?*

— *How do you think others see you because of what you say or don't say, do or don't do?*

Shame and doing the right thing

So how do we get integrity? Is there a gene for it or is it, as I believe, something that must be nurtured and that grows over time, like wisdom. To explore this, I would like to refer back to my work and study in the field of restorative justice.

One of the many interesting things I do is to train school management and teachers to better manage incidents of harmful behaviour by students (such as bullying, violence, classroom disruption, theft and destruction of property). Part of the training program mandates that the school examines current practice and the thinking, beliefs and values that underpin behaviour management (there are links between how they do this, school climate and crime prevention for young people).

Clearly, much of what we do in schools is shaped by our beliefs that punishment is the best way to change behaviour. But John Braithwaite, an eminent Australian criminologist, suggests that when examining compliance (and the lack of it), it is fruitful to explore the following question: *Why it is that most kids (and adults) do the right thing most of the time?* So, of course, I ask this question of participants in my training programs. These are the usual answers I receive about why we comply; that is, what influences us to do the right thing:

— socialisation about ethics, morals and values, usually a product of upbringing, religion, school
— conscience; it feels right; knowing the difference between right and wrong
— beliefs about 'do unto others'
— it's easier to do the right thing than the wrong; there are rewards for doing the right thing
— fear of consequences: loss of liberty, income and fines
— fear of disappointing significant others or being excluded.

Braithwaite proposes a sociological view of these influences and has concluded that *shame* plays a significant role in the development of that mechanism which we call conscience—our sense of right and wrong.

A sociological view

In our early years, we come to fear the disapproval of those of significance (family), as our wrongdoing places stress on these relationships and therefore our very survival. Of course, as we age and our relationships expand outside family, public disapproval exerts an increasingly greater influence. Braithwaite calls this social and *external* regulator of our behaviour *Disgrace Shame*.

As our sense of right and wrong is shaped and strengthened, we are able to better control our own behaviour (as our locus of control moves from external to internal). We learn to exercise discretion—an *internal* regulator, which Braithwaite calls *Discretion Shame*. This is our conscience at work.

So it would seem that *conscience* depends on the influences and experiences we have had, which in turn determine what we believe and value; and on the strength of the relationships we have had with those who are significant in our lives, and the strength of our fear of disappointing them.

Pangs of conscience and feelings of guilt are effective deterrents. Relationships matter. Strong connections are vital to our emotional and physical wellbeing. If you have been lucky enough to fall under the influence of family or significant others to whom integrity is a life value, then you might just grow some yourself.

A biological view

Braithwaite's view of shame is sociological. Shame, via the development of conscience, is a social regulator. An alternative view was presented by Silvan S Tomkins in his work on Affect and Script Theory (the word *affect,* in this context, describes a biological pattern of events that is triggered by a stimulus). Tomkins proposed a biological mechanism for affects (such as shame, fear, anger, excitement, enjoyment) that governs our behaviour and motivation. The theory is very complex, and any simplification I give here is fraught with the danger of inaccuracy. However, I think it is important to try (and see 'For further exploration' at the end of this chapter if you would like to learn more about this topic).

Charles Darwin believed that the mechanisms that govern our feelings and emotions are innate. He suggested that affective expressions evolved primarily to prepare the organism for action, and so play a role in motivation.

Tomkins built on the work of Darwin, and suggested that we have evolved an affect system in the brain for the purpose of simplifying the large amount of stimulus we receive (information from our eyes, ears and skin; smell, touch, pain, thoughts and so on). We are 'wired' to discern between, and respond to, the many inputs that call for our attention at any moment.

An affect (shame, fear, excitement and so on) produces an urgent, distinctive, qualitative experience that causes us to care about what is happening to us—this is a *biologically triggered* mechanism. Our body responds to an affect with an appropriate physiological response (such as changes in breathing and heart rate, blood flow to the skin or adrenalin surges). The face is the best place to observe which affect is triggered at any given moment. This is because the face's musculature, blood flow and nerve development are complicated and finely tuned. (In fact, in the years since Tomkins's work, there has been a great deal of research on the face, its display of affect and what this tells us about the emotional life of a person, their character and trustworthiness.)

When we become aware of an affect, it is called a *feeling*. Our emotions are shaped by our experiences of an affect and the ways others have reacted to that affect throughout our lifetime. For example, the sum total of all of our experience with the emotion anger, from birth onwards, determines our individual way of expressing anger. This is why one person will rage and throw things when angry, while another will simply clamp down on feelings, clench fists and make no verbal display whatsoever. In other words, emotion has an element of *biography*.

Tomkins identified nine affects in total.

Positive affects, which are inherently rewarding:

1. interest–excitement (having fun, being engaged)
2. enjoyment–joy (happy, contented, satisfied, relieved).

A *neutral affect*, which 'clears the decks' and demands we pay attention to anything that might follow:

3. surprise–startle.

Negative affects, which are inherently punishing or 'toxic':

4. fear–terror
5. anger–rage
6. distress–anguish (a steady state caused when things have gone wrong and stayed wrong, such as fatigue, toothache, overload, grief and long-term conflict)
7. dissmell (sense of smell mechanism that allows us to reject something that smells bad and works to protect us from taking in anything which might be toxic)

8. disgust
9. shame–humiliation.

For the purposes of this discussion, it is interesting to examine the role of the negative affect of *disgust*. According to Tomkins, disgust is the mechanism that protects us from the possible excesses of our hunger drive. When we take in food or drink that is, or could be, toxic, disgust causes us to expel the substance by spitting or even vomiting it out. Think of the look on the face of someone who has tasted something awful—that is disgust! Disgust signifies *rejection after sampling*. In a relationship sense, disgust is what happens when we have taken someone into our lives and trusted them, and they have ultimately disappointed us; let us down. We even have language for this: someone, something or a situation 'makes us sick', is 'really disgusting' or, if it's bad enough, is 'revolting'.

How does this relate to integrity? It demonstrates that disgust is a biological mechanism that is linked to lack of trust. If people no longer trust you, they will perform the emotional equivalent of spitting you out in disgust. If you have let them down badly, they will avoid further contact with you. They will avoid you in disgust—rejection after sampling!

The second affect of interest is *shame–humiliation*. Like Braithwaite, though from a very different perspective, Tomkins described shame as a social regulator. The shame mechanism is triggered when anything interferes with the two positive affects (interest and enjoyment). He suggests that shame's evolutionary advantage is that it lets us know when positive affect is blocked.

Shame (and its more intense version, humiliation) tells us that something is not right in a particular situation. The shame mechanism is triggered when our connections with others are under threat (although, in adults, it can sometimes be difficult to identify; we may experience shame as a feeling of distance or isolation from, or rejection by, another). This is part of the biological advantage that shame gives us if we wish to live our lives in a positive way.

Shame in the workplace

Our connections with each other are critical to our sense of belonging, to our survival. Shame let's us know that connections are damaged. Knowing that shame has been triggered allows us, if we have the courage and skills, to explore what has gone wrong and then make it right.

There are times, however, when we are unable to repair a damaged connection. This may be because of the particular circumstances of the situation. More often, though, it is because of negative patterns of response we have learned in order to diminish the emotional impact of shame. Don Nathanson has identified a 'library' of scripts for these patterns of response. He calls this the *compass of shame* (see figure 3.1). We all carry some baggage (scripts) from the early influences of family, school and community, and sometimes these scripts include unhealthy ways to avoid shame, fear and distress, as illustrated. And we all know how powerful that baggage can be in our workplaces.

Figure 3.1 The compass of shame

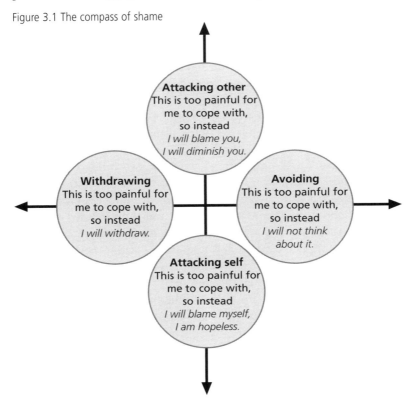

Think about how you react when your connections with others are damaged (that is, shame is triggered).

— *Where do you sit on the compass?*

— *Is your response different for family? Work? Friends? Your boss? Your peers?*

— *What baggage do you carry that leads you to respond in these ways?*

— *What about those around you? What is their response to shame?*

In my work, I have observed that certain actions that trigger (often deliberately) the shame response are always present in chronically toxic workplaces. These actions include:

- abuse and criticism
- letting people down (also induces disgust)
- office gossip, backstabbing and 'white-anting'
- bullying and harassment
- poor management of performance reviews
- poor management process
- lack of engagement, explanation and clarity of expectation.

Think about all the difficult scenarios and behaviours in your workplace. Think about how uncomfortable people feel and how they respond as they seek to limit the emotional impact of shame. This will give you an inkling of the impact of shame on levels of job satisfaction and productivity. High levels of conflict that have existed for weeks, months and sometimes years mean that there is probably a climate of chronic shame; and because things have gone wrong and stayed wrong, a climate of chronic distress.

Jane's story

From a colleague, Jane, in Washington, DC.

I recently worked for a corporation that had a contract with a government agency here in DC. I will keep its identity anonymous (although I would love to complain and 'diss' it). Suffice it to say it is now going to be in the Homeland Security Department.

The tactics of shaming that were used on both the corporate side and the government side were shocking. It actually did more to push me to honour my interest in working with shame than anything I've experienced (outside of my own personal history). The tactics used in this type of scenario were all about power and control of others—it is what these lousy managers seemed to 'get off on'.

Tactics used were:

Worker bees are invisible. *For example, the corporate manager getting together with the team leader from government and me (the worker bee) to discuss something—and talking about me as if I was not sitting there. If I did say something it was not 'taken in' or acknowledged.*

Lack of deference. *For example, I was talked about and my work was talked about at a high level meeting as if I was not there. Later I was told that it was a bad management decision to even have me there!*

Secrecy. *In DC (and elsewhere?) the rule is that 'information is power'. I have information means I have power . . . and, what is more, I have power over you (after all you are in the dark); you don't have this information so you will not be able to move in the direction that I know we are going in. (Think about how shaming this is: it sets people up to be embarrassed, to look stupid, to look awkward, to be ridiculous).*

Control (and control over). *This manifests in all the rules and regulations. What this says is: 'You are not trusted. How you spend your time is not trusted.' You are logged in, logged out. Lots of musts.*

Follow the party line. *Here the manager is super loyal to all policies even though it strangles creativity and creates strife among employees.*

Focus on money, *rather than best product, best work environment. Attitude that the bottom line is paramount. People are secondary.*

Hypocrisy *(opposite of congruency). They say people are first, but they are not. Includes the manager being falsely or overly solicitous and condescending.*

Management through intimidation and fear. *If you don't do this, x will happen (x is bad).*

Misuse of employees' time. *Huge lack of deference, especially for employees who gain satisfaction out of being productive (as studies show that most of us do). For example, several times I took the shuttle to our downtown office for a meeting, only to find the meeting cancelled because the team leader had received incorrect information from her management. This tactic includes cancelling projects half way through or changing midstream (flexible is good but continually sending people down the wrong alley is damaging).*

False pride used to shame. *The attitude of: I am the boss and don't you ever forget it.*

So, it is important to identify when the shame mechanism is operating, in yourself and others, so you can set about repairing relationships and creating a healthy workplace environment.

The key to healthy workplaces

It is not for nothing that the development of emotional intelligence involves the capacity to self-reflect—to understand self—before being able to understand others! Which is why integrity has such a strong role to play if you wish to develop and maintain emotionally healthy relationships in your workplace.

The people you manage and lead need to know what you stand for (your values) and where you are taking them (the goals of the organisation and for their own work). You must demonstrate that you are reliable, honest and trustworthy and that you walk your talk. They need to see your values in action, that you value healthy relationships and that you have their best interests at heart. They need to see that you value openness and honesty in interpersonal transactions. They need to know that they will not be deliberately diminished by your actions.

In other words, to maintain healthy relations with those you lead, you must act with integrity. If these things don't happen, people will experience disgust and shame, often felt as confusion and anxiety, betrayal, rejection and isolation. They will get sick. They will resign or make trouble. How can anyone possibly imagine that people can do their best work under these conditions? In the end, a lack of the old fashioned virtue of integrity will cost the organisation dearly.

Tomkins and others after him have clearly defined the necessary conditions for developing emotionally healthy relationships. The outcomes sought are very straightforward—to maximise positive affect and minimise negative affect. To achieve this, the rules are very simple—this is not rocket science. (I hope Tomkins, from his grave, will forgive my spin on this blueprint.)

- Develop a cultural climate where it is acceptable to be open and honest and to talk about how we feel. This is called the mutualisation of affect.
- Find ways to validate, listen to, take seriously and respect others' negative views or feelings and refrain from 'blowing people

off'. When we are truly listened to and taken seriously, and feel understood and valued, negative affect is minimised.

- Discourage harmful workplace policies, practices and behaviours that diminish others, such as disrespect, bad manners, poor customer service, dishonesty, bullying and abuse. Minimise instances of behaviour that causes negative affect.
- Encourage mutually interesting and satisfying work, and work practices, and give clear direction that provides staff with clarity and a sense of security. Maximise positive affect.

Deliberate development of a climate of integrity, openness and honesty provides the necessary conditions for the development of emotionally respectful relationships.

Joe's story

Joe works as a therapist and counsellor with AIDS/HIV patients.

A manager with integrity is authentic—that is, they are who and what they are and don't hide behind a role that sets them above others or covertly manipulates their subordinates. They are honest and direct. In our field we might say they are congruent. What's on the inside is displayed on the outside.

Good managers know how to collaborate with those they manage. That means they listen to all input and have the judgement and leadership to decide on a course of action after all the data are in and then mobilise and motivate their team to work together, utilising the strengths of each member.

They are both 'task oriented' and 'emotionally intelligent', because they know that the work will get done when people 'feel' their best as valued and important members of the project. They affirm the strengths of their workers and are sincerely interested in helping people to grow in areas of weakness. Thus, they see to it that there are opportunities for growth and advancement in each person's skill set.

Leadership and integrity

Most serious writers on leadership have something to say about integrity, although some mention it only in passing and without exploration of its meaning. Others give it the seriousness it deserves.

In his book *Secrets of Effective Leadership: A Practical Guide to*

Success, Fred Manske clearly honours the virtue of integrity. His advice includes:

- Hire leaders who practise high principles; that is, live by the highest standards of honesty and integrity.
- Once such leaders are in place at all levels of the organisation, ensure 'frequent, candid information'. Continued sharing of both good and bad news builds trust, the other key to effective organisations. Employees are well aware that everything won't always be rosy. From the launching pad of honest exchange between leader and follower, an organisation can do the right things right and prosper in the process.

In his article, 'Values-based leadership has huge pay-off', Jim Clemmer reminds us that:

. . . most organisations, management teams, and managers have a major gulf between what they say and what they do. Since they confuse their aspired behaviour with their actual behaviour, they don't recognise their own rhetoric—reality gulf. Sometimes they point to declining work ethic as a reason for the inconsistent behaviour on their team or in their organisation.

But that is often a cop-out. The desire for doing meaningful work, being part of a winning team, and making a difference in our job has been on a steady increase throughout the Western world. If I feel that 'people don't want to work any more' I need to take a deep look in my management mirror. Maybe they just don't want to work with me.

In *Do You Know If You Are Trusted*, Michael Maccoby says:

Highly educated employees don't trust information unless they know its meaning for them. It is not enough to communicate the information with talks and memos . . . employees need to be able to question directives, and managers need to be open about their reasoning, why they made their decisions . . . Creating trust requires interactive communication, dialogue based on values of respect and continual learning. Employees also need to trust that management will not punish mistakes or criticism but will use them as basis for learning.

Kouzes and Posner in *The Leadership Challenge* devote an entire chapter, 'Set the example: Doing what you say you will do', to the development of integrity (although they don't call it that). It's a powerful read. In their own research on leader credibility (a component of integrity), they asked: how do you know if someone is credible; can credibility be defined in behavioural terms; and how do you recognise credible leaders? Not surprisingly, the most frequent response was: 'They do what they say they will do'. People listen to the talk, watch the walk and then decide whether there is congruence. In setting an example there must be clarity around their values (the 'say') and then they must act on their beliefs (the 'do').

Kouzes and Postner also advise that these *beliefs and values must be shared*. What they mean by this is:

- Personal values and beliefs and those of others must be shared.
- Constituents are unified around shared values.
- Attention is paid constantly to how self and others are living the values.

They discuss values in the following way:

Values help us to determine what to do and what not to do. They're the deep seated, pervasive standards that influence every aspect of our lives: our moral judgements, our responses to others, our commitments to personal and organisational goals. Values set the parameters for the hundreds of decisions we make every day. Options that run counter to our value systems are seldom acted upon; and if they are, it's done with a sense of compliance rather than commitment. Values contribute to our personal 'bottom line'.
Kouzes and Postner

Sound familiar? Echoes of Braithwaite's development of conscience and the discretion–shame mechanisms, and Tomkins's scripts for the management of our affects/emotions.

A word of warning, though, about values. Various researchers have found that not everyone agrees about the *meaning* of a value. One researcher found 185 different behavioural expectations around the value of integrity alone! It is the *process of dialogue* about meaning that is important (number one in Tomkins's blueprint for an emotionally healthy climate); that is, open and honest talk about how we feel, our values, what has happened, what's working, what's not, actions aligning with the organisation's values and our own.

In its *Tools for Developing Successful Executives* (360-degree feedback), the Centre for Creative Leadership lists a number of factors and attributes that can derail an executive's career. I'll include the full list here, but want you to note the references to the items that I think contribute to a lack of integrity (my emphasis added in italics):

- *insensitive to others*
- *cold, aloof, arrogant*
- *overly ambitious*
- *lack of composure*
- failing to staff effectively
- *over-managing*
- inability to think strategically
- *betrayal of trust*
- low detail orientation
- *over-dependence on an advocate/mentor*
- over-dependence on a single skill
- inability to adapt to bosses/strategies/management culture
- performance problems with business
- key skill deficiencies.

Of course, not all developing leaders have black holes in all 14 areas. But it is interesting to see that the research does list those 'soft' skills related to emotional intelligence that seem to impact on integrity or the lack of it.

Lombado and Eichinger, in their book, *What To Do Before It's Too Late*, found that organisations often derail managers by giving little feedback about 'how you did it', concentrating rather on 'what you did'. Many managers got their first 'how you did it' feedback only after they were derailed.

We struggle to give feedback to those who lead and manage us, to our peers and to those we lead. This is very human, and very unfortunate. We know that the experience will be one of shame—for them and for us. Culturally, we are not good at it. It is rare to find it modelled effectively. Yet the failure of management to give employees honest feedback is one of the greatest shortcomings in the workplace. Managers especially avoid giving feedback that concerns matters that impact on relationships—usually people behaving inappropriately, being too slack, aggressive or abusive, or not taking responsibility. These managers have failed in their duty of care. And *their* managers have failed them for not demanding that they do this hard work. My experience is that, more often than not, performance management is done very poorly, and the cost in down time, low morale and poor productivity is massive.

With a *restorative* approach to problem solving (as opposed to a blaming approach)—with the emphasis on exploring the harm that has been done—management and employees alike are invited to tell their stories, take responsibility for their part in the doing of damage, and eventually cooperate to develop a way forward that involves repairing the harm and minimising the likelihood of it occurring in the future. This is integrity at work in a group setting, no less. But getting people used to the idea that it's alright to talk honestly in their daily transactions with each other is hard work. We are simply not used to it.

I don't wish to labour the point or state the obvious, but I think it's necessary to be very clear that *integrity and positive relationships are closely linked*. You simply cannot get the best from your employees or colleagues unless you are trusted; you walk your talk and are open and honest in your dealings with them. This means that one of your values must be 'relationships are important'; that is, the recognition that positive relationships lie at the heart of your organisation's success.

So, exercising integrity will make a difference to your relationships with others, job satisfaction, productivity and your organisation's bottom line. Your leadership behaviour must demonstrate this virtue in a genuine way. People pay attention to what you say and do.

And imagine what could be achieved if you actively and deliberately recruited leaders, managers and staff with integrity?

Becoming a leader of integrity

In naming those leaders in our professional or personal lives who have stood the integrity test, it is clear that it is a quality that, while respected, is rare. From a sociological and biological perspective, it seems that the getting of integrity is determined by the kinds of influences we have been exposed to over time. But I think it's also fair to say that each of us is a 'work in progress'. The shaping of a person's qualities and character is surely a lifetime job, rather than the result of some static genetic trait like blue eyes or height. Of course, there are those who claim 'well, that's just the way I am', implying that change is not possible. I believe this is a cop-out, and an excuse for not doing the hard work needed to do things differently.

So, for me, integrity is more of a journey than a destination. I don't think I'm there yet. I'm not old enough for a start. I'm still learning.

I didn't ask my focus group whether they thought *I* had integrity, because I didn't want to put them on the spot (and, perhaps, was not ready to hear their answers). I do know, however, that when I have worked for, and with, good people who are clear about their values and beliefs, will not deviate under pressure, cannot be corrupted, and examine their hearts and conscience for answers in difficult times, I have become a better person and, therefore, do better work.

Can we learn integrity from coursework? Unlikely. The Centre for Creative Leadership has conducted extensive research on learning, growth and development and how they impact on careers. They advise that 'other people' are the best source of learning for this virtue and this substantiates the sociological and biological theory mentioned earlier in this chapter. But there are some things we can do to make the journey easier. Here are some of my suggestions (and you will find a summary of these points at the end of the chapter).

- Understand that your integrity in dealings with others (and yourself) is an essential component of the glue in your relationships. It delivers respect, loyalty, commitment and trust. It's a virtue worthy of your interest.
- Find role models who are known for their integrity and watch their values playing out. Watch their behaviour. Learn from their example how they 'do' honesty and openness, how they walk their talk.
- Watch someone who is a spectacular failure at integrity and *don't* follow in his or her footsteps.
- Find someone known for his or her integrity to coach and mentor you. Listen to their views and values. Ask them about what integrity means to them. Talk to their staff (with permission) about the quality of their relationships with their staff. Learn from them how to do it. Find out *how* they go about deciding what to say and do when the pressure is on. How do they wrestle with their sense of right and wrong?

- Seriously examine these questions. What do you believe in? What are your values about right and wrong? How did you learn them? What has influenced how you deal with people?
- Engage your staff in dialogue about how they feel about the issues that affect them. Talk about integrity generally. Find out how important it is to them. Ask them how they feel when they are let down.
- Seek feedback about your staff's perceptions of your integrity—whether or not they trust you to walk your talk. Do they know (and understand) your talk?
- Have courage. Integrity is hard work. Be prepared to be disadvantaged sometimes when you make a stand over an issue, or to be inconvenienced when you made a promise.
- Be prepared to take the risk of changing the way you deal with others, and yourself.
- Do what you say you will do. Don't let people down.

Conclusion

So if integrity is so important, why isn't there more of it around?

I suspect that the 'me' generation has made a priority of self-interest. I think the pursuit of profit at all costs has seduced us away from our responsibilities to our relationships with others. We are on the move. The ease of mobility means our connections with others are weaker—and so, therefore, are our obligations. Families and communities have become disconnected. How many of us know our neighbours well? Or care about them? Career progress no longer means staying in the same company for a lifetime. Company loyalty is a short-term phenomenon. The loyalty and respect of workmates for us seems to matter less. I shudder to think of what effect all of this will have on our young people who are new to employment, and who look to us for guidance and example.

Integrity takes courage, but I don't need to remind you about what's at stake if we don't have a go at it.

Sometimes it's too hard. I can think of key moments in my own professional and personal life when I failed the test and damaged relationships that I valued at the time. To this day, I remain ashamed of those moments, but the shame serves to keep me straight for the next time around. The internal conflict is too uncomfortable for me to make those mistakes again.

A final story

This story is about John Goggin, a boss of mine from my time at Queensland Education.

John was a high school principal and then a senior public servant. He retired recently from the public service, but is busier than ever in his new life as a consultant. I worked with John during a time of massive restructuring that was confusing and hurtful for most involved.

John ran a tight ship in our district office. He was and is an incredibly hard worker. He demanded the highest standards of client service from us. He was honest and open in his dealings with us. He tuned us up when we needed it. He never kept us in the dark. He did what he said he would do. He was committed to our wellbeing. He stood up for our interests and for us. He encouraged our career development.

He was not always popular with his own line managers as he fought the good fight. He was probably too honest and had not mastered the art of ducking and weaving in a highly political climate in order to fulfil his own career aspirations. I know those career disappointments hurt him. But he would never sacrifice our interests for the sake of his own.

The man had integrity . . . we trusted him . . . and I would have walked over hot coals for him.

Seven tips for developing integrity

1 Value integrity.
2 Talk about integrity.
3 Find an integrity mentor.
4 Seek feedback.
5 Examine your heart.
6 Be courageous.
7 Walk your talk.

For further exploration

—J Braithwaite, *Crime, Shame and Reintegration,* Cambridge University Press, Cambridge, 1989.
This definitive text distinguishes between shaming that is reintegrative and shaming that is stigmatising.

—Center for Creative Leadership, *Tools for Developing Successful Executives,* Center for Creative Leadership, Greensboro, 1997.
CCL is one of the leading trainers and research institutes for the development of leadership in executives and managers.

—EV Demos, *Exploring Affect: The Selected Writings of Silvan S Tomkins,* Cambridge University Press, Cambridge, 1995.
This is a very useful volume that contains extracts from Tomkins's work on Affect and Script Theory, his model of human behaviour and motivation, and how we make sense of the world. Please note, the works of Silvan S Tomkins are extremely complex and not for the faint hearted!

—VC Kelly Jr, 'Affect and the redefinition of intimacy', in DL Nathanson (ed.), *Knowing Feeling,* WW Norton, New York, 1996.
While written primarily as a guide for counselling couples, its material contains important insights about relationships in general that can be easily extrapolated into the workplace.

—DL Nathanson, *Shame and Pride: Affect, Sex, and the Birth of Self,* WW Norton, New York, 1992.
A brilliantly readable text that introduces Silvan Tomkins's work on Affect and Script Theory to a broader readership, and adds many ideas of his own developed from his professional life as a medical practitioner and psychiatrist.

—DL Nathanson, 'About emotion', in DL Nathanson (ed.), *Knowing Feeling,* WW Norton, New York, 1996.
This is a very helpful chapter on Affect Theory for those who don't want to read an entire textbook on the subject!

For further information on restorative justice, try the following sites:

—H Zehr and H Mika, Fundamental Concepts of Restorative Justice, at www.ojp.usdoj.gov/nij/rest-just/ch1/fundamental.html

—Restorative Practices Library, www.restorativepractices.org

—Restorative Justice (my own site) www.thorsborne.com.au

COMPASSION   **4**

Fabian Dattner

About the author

Fabian Dattner BA (Hons) (Sociology)

Fabian Dattner is a well-known social entrepreneur, author, much-sought-after speaker, visionary and change agent.

She is founding partner of Dattner Grant, a specialist consultancy working in leadership development and high-order strategic processes. She is a frequent commentator on leadership issues on radio and in the press and was included in Susan Mitchell's *Tall Poppies Too* and in her recent book on eight Australian women, *Split the World Apart*.

Fabian is well known for her work in both community and organisational change and as a passionate advocate for a more inclusive style of leadership towards greater social and environmental accountability. She is also an experienced business advocate with a keen understanding of the challenges operating in a complex and competitive commercial market. Her clients include organisations as diverse as AGL, Aurora Tasmania, EPA, The Wilderness Society, Mittagong Forum, Fox Home Entertainment, Thrifty and Australian Red Cross Blood Bank.

Her company runs a number of programs for women in, or about to take up, leadership roles; and for young people in years 11 and 12 (the Custodian Program), helping them to change and not just be changed by the world they find themselves in.

Fabian is the author of *Naked Truth: an Open Letter to the Australian Working Community* (Allen & Unwin) and *Nothing Ventured, Nothing Gained* (Penguin). She is the co-author of *The Three Spirits of Leadership: The United Voice of the Entrepreneur, the Corporation and the Community* (Allen & Unwin), and is currently completing a Masters degree in Vocational Education.

Fabian Dattner can be reached at fabian@dattnergrant.com.au.

Introduction

We shall not cease from exploration, and the end of all our exploring will be to return to the place where we started, and know it for the first time.

TS Eliot in *Four Quartets*

Truly great leadership is the art and science of understanding a 'divine language called the spirit of life'. It is about the courage and personal flexibility necessary to counsel wisely in a turbulent, uncertain, changeable world. It is about the intuitive sense of possibility that comes from broad knowledge that gives rise, in itself, to a sense of probability. It is about the will to act, that translates intentions into measurable, durable, sustainable outcomes that improve the lot of all.

Fabian Dattner, discussing a quote from Pierre-Jean Fabre

The concept of 'compassion' is hard to reduce to words. Like 'love' it is all-embracing; known when it is apparent; and known when it is absent. It may prove to be 'untutorable', being the outcome of the passage of time and of emerging wisdom rather than known or learned fact. Yet in saying this, I know that it is greatly wanting in our world today. We are clever as a species, perhaps never more overtly so; but we are not compassionate with one another, at least not as often as we want or need to be.

Compassion is measured by our ability as individuals and as leaders to see the world through another's eyes, to understand what motivates another human being, what gives them joy and what weighs them down. It is about service not selfishness. It is emotional alchemy—instead of the transmutation of base metals into gold it is the transformation of human potential into shared, enabling outcomes for all.

Compassion is not empathy (although it embraces this); it is not sympathy (although at times this is evident); it is not kindness (though kindness is its cornerstone); it is not passion (yet passion is its fuel); and it is not a sign of weakness (for it is only exercised by truly great and generous leaders).

When leaders demonstrate compassion, it is evident in their commitment to shared purpose, aligned values, common understanding, and a clear and engaging direction. It is compassion that enables leaders to provide long-term solutions that help to build human community, not to destroy it. Compassion extends to all that is around us; the miracle of what the earth contains and the practical reality that we cannot survive without it.

Compassion is the ability of leaders to listen to both the vocal and the inarticulate and, having listened, to act with wisdom. It is the middle path, embodying synergy, not the paths on the extreme that are lived out in win/lose, right/wrong battles of attrition.

Compassion is a leadership virtue and a worthy aspiration, but it is not an easy one.

The lure of reductionism

It seems to me that much of what it is to be human has been turned into academic process; something to be analysed, synthesised, reduced to its component parts, and only then understood and valued. We assume that all things can be unpacked, and in the unpacking, we will achieve clarity. We determinedly and intentionally uncloak mystery until it is no longer mysterious and we believe that this process will make us wiser, and our world more controllable. It is the paradox of being human, part of our greatness and part of our folly.

To be fair, it is an important part of our journey . . . but it is not all of it. Our trust in the uncloaking process is at the expense of a more intuited wisdom, of which compassion is elemental. Despite the allure of the unveiling, we persist at our peril.

In 1991, in the Arizona desert, there was a famous experiment called *Biosphere II*. The intention of this expensive showcase (some US$200 million in the making) was to demonstrate mankind's mastery over our physical domain. Eight people were sealed in an enormous dome, in which were built replicas of a variety of Earth's ecosystems—a modern day Noah's Ark if you will. It failed, miserably and quickly, and whilst a great deal of media attention was focused on its building and its sealing, little emerged from its collapse. Essentially, only a few curious desert creatures and a group of frustrated scientists witnessed the final curtain call, despite the world's attention for opening night. Today, looking back, perhaps more than anything else it was a warning to us not to over-simplify life, not to think that by reducing complexity to its constituent parts we can recreate the whole.

The reductionist theory—engaging, informing and enlightening as it is for human beings—is not enough. It never will be. Things are not simple, despite our dearest wish that they could be so. In fact, in a frantic attempt to simplify and contain the world around us, it is possible we are generating even more complexity and losing control. Perhaps we have fooled ourselves into believing that there is a right and wrong way to 'do life', and so making mistakes is about wrong process and failure, rather than about learning. I believe the repercussions of this are evident everywhere in our natural world.

The repercussions of reductionism are also apparent in the emerging issues for the human community. In the developed West, we have had a predisposition to look only at the individual parts of what makes us tick emotionally, physically, intellectually— whether we are under the analyst's gaze, or in the hands of the organisational re-engineer. We have become obsessed with efficiency and effectiveness and how to live life more profitably. In the process of improving systems and methodology, however, we have somehow undervalued the rich and complex tapestry of human relationships. Not only does this process potentially threaten the very stability of the environment which sustains life, it also undermines how we see each other on a macro scale (in terms of the increasingly yawning divide between the 'haves' and the 'have nots') and on a micro scale (in terms of destroying the concept of 'we' by rewarding the endeavours and focus of 'I').

With this in mind, I believe that if we are, in time, to fulfil our potential, then leadership will have to include:
- acting as stewards for the human community
- re-engaging trust
- nurturing relationships
- accepting responsibility for our ecological footprints
- protecting the inheritance of our children
- respecting and valuing biological diversity.

Unpacking the mystery of existence will not necessarily help us to do this, though it may be a valuable (some might say unstoppable) element of the process. It is our over-reliance on unpacking, unveiling and reducing that is our enemy. It makes us deaf to human entreaty, which includes the voices of our loved ones as much as the people who follow our lead.

A more holistic (to use a somewhat hackneyed word) approach to leadership, then, may be about valuing 'intuited wisdom' and about 'right action'. Kindness, as much as cleverness, will be the measure of our effectiveness.

In this journey, I believe the crucial, though perhaps not obvious, ingredient for sustained success will be *compassion*. Without compassion, the recipe fails over and over again. With compassion (and despite the absence of other ingredients that in the past we have assumed were essential) humanity can rise against extraordinary adversity and apparently insurmountable odds—and win. This is true for communities, countries and families. Surprisingly, it is also true for business.

New ways of leading

My own leadership journey has been a variable and bumpy ride; sometimes jubilant, sometimes frustrating and intimidating. I have had, and continue to have, periods of great success and periods where I wonder at my own competency and right to be a leader. I recognise it is a challenging, tough, frequently isolating role to take up in life, so I do not offer advice lightly to leaders.

Today, leaders are struggling to come to terms with increasing organisational effectiveness, sustaining morale in challenging times, engaging in the sort of communication that ensures accurate data and supports climate, building innovation, improving systems, developing meaningful purpose, making quality decisions *and* engaging and retaining the right people. We are being tested to the very boundaries of human willingness. Leadership, and doing it well, isn't easy.

Yet leadership is one of the most studied of human jurisdictions. Those who study leadership and how we 'do' it generally divide into the following camps:

- *Trait* theory—if we can identify the right traits of leadership, innate in the individual, then we will be able to guarantee greatness.
- *Behaviour* and *style* theories—what leaders actually do, and therefore can be trained to do, rather than what they are genetically endowed with.

- A range of *situational* and *contingency* theories—intense scrutiny of the situation and the skills a leader requires to produce the best outcomes in a specific situation; and developing contingencies when situations change.

Others have totally ditched leadership models, saying it simply isn't that easy. I am in this last category.

Everything I know about leadership (and I've spent the best part of the last 20 years living and breathing it every waking moment of every day) tells me that a way of looking at leadership is emerging that is kinder on all of us—leader and follower alike (and we may be both at various times). Although it will build on all we have learned about leadership so far, it will also take us back to our roots. It will remind us of what it meant once upon a time to be *stewards and custodians*, responsible for genuinely sustaining and leading community, not just aggregating stories of personal success (measured by our own individual badges of honour—personal wealth and its symbols).

Compassion is critical to this journey, but it is a tricky guiding light. It does not lend itself nicely to division or reduction. It can't be put under the microscope, clearly defined, then coached and developed (not even when it is attributed as a response in a particular part of the brain to a particular sequence of stimulations). This is not because compassion is not open to such analysis, but because the very process of analysis will make us blind to it, destroy its mystery and hence its power over our decisions and actions. As the Buddhists say, if you have to define enlightenment, then you do not understand it.

Compassionate leadership, and the responsibilities it entails, will be seen by many to be neither pragmatic nor hard-nosed enough. Nice if you have the luxury of time on your side but, realistically, not workable in the competitive, changeable and technology-driven world in which we operate. Given our recent economic rationalist, reductionish experiences, this is an understandable lens through which to filter reality, but it doesn't make it real and it certainly doesn't make it sustainable.

For those who like data, let me take you on a brief data journey and, in the process, put forward a commercially compelling reason to integrate compassion into how we lead and influence others.

Over the last three years, my organisation has conduced *honesty audits* in some 30 Australian businesses. These audits have involved interviews with over 1800 Australians. Amongst other things, the honesty audit process enables leaders to hear the human story in their own organisations (government, not-for-profit, corporate and entrepreneurial); what aids people to do their best and what undermines them; how they see leadership; and what they wish leaders would do differently.

I developed the process many years ago, frustrated at the predisposition in organisational research to reduce how we feel about coming to work to a series of statistical patterns. Over the past 14 years, we have interviewed thousands of people, leaders and followers alike. The interviews of the past three years, however, have really highlighted for me the need for leaders to take the emergent themes seriously. The following is an outline of those themes that are relevant to this discussion of the role of compassion in leadership and organisations.

To begin with the more positive results:

- **People are the key strength.** 83 per cent of organisations rated people as their key strength. Over and over again we were told of the value of effort, commitment, dedication, knowledge and teamwork. Despite an insecure environment and low levels of employee trust for leaders, people—either individually or in teams—were seen to be the backbone of modern endeavour.

- **Organisational reputation is valued.** In 66 per cent of organisations, employees felt that the reputation of the organisation was critical to their level of commitment. This was about alignment of values; a sense that the organisation was there for the long haul and that individual and collective actions would contribute to a journey bigger than any given individual (in many instances this was despite, not because of, leadership).

- **Product or service is valued.** In 55 per cent of organisations, staff said it was the product or service that was most keenly valued. 'What we do or sell is important to us. If we feel it genuinely adds value, then the challenge of making meaning out of our own lives is easier.'

Beyond this, strengths were few and inconsistent, but issues (or weaknesses if I am to be honest) mounted an unarguable case for change.

When interviewees were asked to identify the issues that undermined the organisation's effectiveness, the results were:

- 76 per cent—lack of, or poor, leadership (critically, both leaders and employees alike identified this as the single biggest issue)
- 66 per cent—lack of visionary objectives
- 45 per cent—lack of aligned purpose and values
- 41 per cent—lack of congruence between the stated values and the observable behaviours of leaders.

Whilst obviously there was much else that emerged from the research, the following issues are critical for organisations. They underpin the case for the value and place of compassion in leadership.

- Leaders feel ill-equipped to lead in the current environment. They and the people they lead recognise the value of leadership (fixed or situational) but feel, in too many instances, that the leaders' skills and focus are outmoded.
- From an employee's perspective, we have become obsessed with explaining *how* to do what we do (system, process, methodology) but not *why* (visionary goals and purpose) and in the absence of a clear and compelling *why*, leadership has become opportunistic and short-term in its focus.
- Many interviewees expressed real anger, frustration and, ultimately, lack of respect for a leadership whose behaviour and rhetoric simply didn't match (for instance, saying that people are our most important asset, then promptly cutting people out of the picture when things get tough). Generally, people were not against the strength of an individual leader's position or values. What they hated (and that is not too strong a word) were leaders who said one thing and then clearly and observably did or rewarded another thing.

What happened to compassion?

In 1995, the government published the *Karpin Report*, several million dollars and a number of years in the making. One of its key conclusions was that Australian leadership needed to invest in its own development. In our own research, the same conclusion emerges, but from follower and leader alike. So, this is not another instance of leader bashing. Far from it. Instead, I think it is a *cri de coeur* (cry of the heart). Followers feel the challenge and see that their leaders are struggling, and at the same time the leaders themselves often feel out of their depth. But why?

Essentially, leadership education in the modern world has supported leaders in improving *how we do* what we do, but this has frequently happened at the expense of *how we feel* about what we do. The Deming revolution (sparked by Edward Deming, the father of the quality movement) developed in the sixties and seventies and reached its climax in the eighties. This revolution was all about improving efficiency and effectiveness. It was part of reductionist thinking. The thinking of the time (embodied a little later in process re-engineering) was that if we could measure what we were doing we could improve it, and this theory was right—for a while. We developed complex organisational planning processes and learned how to manage the 'doing' of business with a high degree of precision. We focused on integrated systems, clearer organisational goals, quality strategic and tactical planning, concise articulation of critical success factors and key performance indicators, and measurement of everything that could be measured.

If we were very good at planning, we made sure individual performance plans were comprehensively linked, measured and regularly assessed according to these agreed deliverables. We incrementally trialled, reviewed, improved, reflected, measured and then tried again. When something went wrong, or if we didn't deliver the expected results, we unpacked the process and measured again, looking for incremental change based on reliable data.

Generally speaking, as a result of this focus, there was a marked improvement in organisational outcomes. Leaders watched as the bottom line improved, which reinforced this style of leadership. So they got better and better at leading it and doing it, and holding people accountable to this style of measuring success. Then we hit the unforgiving nineties and many organisations 'flat-lined' (they had a 'near death' experience or they died). Many organisations had grown complacent on the back of the dramatic improvements brought about by the quality revolution. However, it was also apparent that the incremental improvements of the quality movement, initiated on the back of the Deming revolution, were insufficient to meet the challenges of the volatile nineties. For many, the dramatic improvements of the sixties, seventies and eighties stopped dead.

Unfortunately, the leaders facing this crisis had been taught that leadership meant concentrating on how to measure, how to look objectively at organisational needs, how to think logically about issues, how to turn off emotions and, above all, how to disengage from the soft people issues. Under pressure, these leaders naturally turned to what had worked for them in the sixties, seventies and eighties; that is, more of the same. As a result, holocausts of cost cutting ensued, under the captaincy of brief heroes such as Al 'Chainsaw' Dunlap. Leaders were told that the problem was not what they were doing, but that they weren't doing enough of it. They weren't lean enough; they had become lazy in their leadership; there wasn't enough focus on minimising costs; they weren't measuring performance or, if they were, weren't monitoring it closely enough. A slash-and-burn leadership focus emerged and toughness became the measure of good leadership.

What it failed to do was count the human cost or the long-term impact to climate (how we all came to *feel* about coming to work) and consequently to consider seeking alternative methods. Instead, the focus (and hence senior leadership rewards) was on short-term restructuring and downsizing—a euphemism for firing a lot of people. Leaders made decisions in the isolation of the boardroom (or on senior leader 'retreats') and often the impact of these decisions was inadequately thought through.

Leaders experienced anxiety and real fear about the commercial consequences of not acting strongly and quickly, and this drove the imperative for downsizing. Alternatives did not easily reveal themselves. Not surprising, considering the leadership model from which such actions emerged.

In many instances, if leaders didn't change or toughen up their behaviour, then young guns who were more than willing to make the hard decisions replaced them. Such sweeping leadership 'cleanouts' implied that the existing leaders were incompetent. However, in reality, the new leaders who replaced them were cast from the same mould; they were just sharper at doing the same things. The new leaders' rewards were short-term and so, all too frequently, were their actions. After all, a slash-and-burn policy will produce short-term results, and the bottom line will quickly show improvements. Senior leaders and directors trained in this model of leadership liked the results, and so the cycle was reinforced. Many such leaders moved on to other organisations before they had time to see the long-term repercussions of their short-term actions.

So Rome burned, and in many places is still burning. The long-term outcomes (organisational, societal and environmental) were all too frequently sacrificed for short-term gains. To be fair, radical cleaning did work for a few organisations (but far fewer than we imagine). In some organisations, internal processes were sloppy, costs were out of kilter with revenue, and the opportunity to move forward was genuinely hampered by incompetent leadership—so severe change was warranted. Their numbers, however, were limited and many organisations were taken on the merry-go-round ride of change, re-engineering and downsizing with little palpable benefit and often measurable harm.

The complete absence of compassion in this picture was often breathtaking and the impact of such strategies was to destroy much that had taken decades to nurture. As we obsessively measured organisational performance on statistical patterns, the human community began to feel raped. Employees, many of whom had been forced to take part in multiple change processes (which all too frequently failed to deliver the promised benefits), stopped trusting their leaders. Staff no longer believed the intentions of management. They felt their opinions were not valued and learned that nothing was secure. 'We', and all that it embodied in terms of history, commitment, effort and contribution, counted for little; 'I' and my ability to look out for myself, counted for much.

This cycle of evolution in modern organisations was marked by our thoughtlessness and our lack of compassion. It bred a level of cynicism and insecurity in people from which we are still trying to recover today.

In some organisations real, measurable improvements occurred but they were not the result of a singular cost-cutting, change-driven, process re-engineering mentality. They were the result of quality leaders who saw business in the round and were not obsessed about any of its parts in isolation. Then, as now, good leaders looked at the whole and, in the process, took human community and organisational intentions forwards, not backwards. Unfortunately, in my experience, they were the exception rather than the rule.

In the late eighties and early nineties, on an almost global basis, we exercised a style of leadership that we may one day look back upon as a dark period in the evolution of our species. Paradoxically, despite the apparent brutishness of much of this behaviour, most leaders of that time were not unkind, selfish or wilful people. For two decades, leaders were trained to do this (and rewarded for it) and many simply lacked the skills to do otherwise.

Unfortunately, we have been slow to get the message that it is a damaging short-term strategy, and this form of leadership continues today in many domains. We are still focused on short-term individual gains at the expense of the long view.

Beyond the status quo of success

Today, in 76 per cent of the organisations we studied, staff and leaders alike recognise that an enormous number of leaders are not equipped to lead in the current environment. They need and are asking for help. The *Karpin Report* identified this in the early nineties and we are once again acknowledging it today. If we are not to remain stuck in Ground Hog Day, we need to do something different. We must recognise that solutions to problems usually don't come from the same environment in which the problems were created.

It is my belief that compassion will be central to our ability to move forward from this place. The lack of meaningful purpose and aligned values is not the conscious consequence of any individual's premeditated unkindness. On the contrary, all individuals—leaders and followers alike—are more effective when there is a *why* for what they do and they feel that who they are, and what they stand for, is aligned with where they find themselves. So, lack of purpose and non-alignment of values is more a comment on *competency* rather than intent. In my experience, people want to do the right thing by one another, and their failure to do so is rarely the consequence of intentional malevolence. It is rather the consequence of lack of choices: 'I know what I want to do, but I fail to do it because I don't actually know how (or am scared) to do what I recognise needs to be done. So, I revert to the known and the familiar.' This in turn leads to inconsistencies between behaviour and rhetoric—what we do and what we say we will do.

Almost by definition, for an individual to rise to the most senior position they must understand how to be successful within the prevailing conditions of the environment in which they are working. Once they are entrenched in a senior position, their continuing success is often (albeit unconsciously) connected to their ability to maintain the status quo.

A change of game plan, however, means a change in the requirements of leadership. This is exactly what is happening today, but many incumbent leaders are ill-equipped to make the necessary change. No familiar alternatives are available, so they hang on to what they know, supporting what is, despite recognising the need to do things differently.

This is part of the *threnody* of compassion—the sad melody at its core, inherent in its application. When people fear failure, they will duck for cover. It is the most natural thing in the world and it is true for all of us. Though this may seem surprisingly obvious, it is rarely taken into account when we plan for change. Understanding this fear is at the centre of compassion.

When we discover a new, successful way of doing things, there is a risk that eventually it will become entrenched as the only way we can do things. When this happens, someone, somewhere will begin to argue a case for the known and the familiar and sticking to it, despite the rhetoric of change, of innovation, of listening and of moving the collective forward.

There is a repetitious pattern in human behaviour, even as we move upwards on our evolutionary spiral. We don't like to admit to failure when our endeavours seem so rich; we don't like admitting we are wrong (even partially so) when we believe ourselves so right; we talk about the power of learning from our mistakes, but we have a tendency to feel our learning reflects failure and so avoid public exposure at all costs (despite rhetoric to the contrary).

Change requires us to enter uncharted waters—where failure can happen, where judgement about an individual's capacity is possible, and where leaders may not fulfil their individual charters. Herein lies the challenge—leaders must change as the evolutionary benchmark is raised, even though they may feel (even unconsciously) that their success is vested in maintaining the status quo.

Today, change is fermenting in every corner of the modern world because of our incredible capacity for inventiveness and, ironically, the very lack of loyalty and commitment bred in the eighties and nineties. Educated and capable people, with no particular attachment to a given organisation or set of collective outcomes, are fuelling constant development and improvement, pursuing change for the sake of change—there is always a better or different way of doing things.

This then demands a new and flexible kind of leadership; alert to people's needs, compassionately responsible for others, and able also to acknowledge the vulnerability of the leader.

Learning to change

All journeys start with a purpose. The purpose empowers us to learn. This is as true of learning to walk as it is of learning to lead in complex environments. Learning, by definition, requires the calibration of action against some future standard or outcome. Learning means that we don't always get it 'right' in the present. We make mistakes, and actively give ourselves permission to make them, as we move forward through the four well-known levels of learning:

1. unconscious incompetence (not knowing the concept of dancing)
2. conscious incompetence (treading on each other's feet as we learn the basic steps to tango)

3. conscious competence (dancing together well, but with someone else still counting out the steps)
4. unconscious competence (gliding through the dance routine with little conscious awareness other than pleasure in the process).

Learning to lead follows the same course, but it happens at different levels—perhaps first as a team leader, then as a project supervisor, a functional manager, a regional leader and then, finally, as a senior leader or director of an organisation. Each level of leadership requires a measure of trial and error. Once attained, each level is then embedded with a level of certainty or unconscious competence—'this is what we must do in order to obtain and retain that measure of success'.

Unfortunately, the level of unconscious competence represents a trap, because to open yourself to learning again is often seen as a step backwards. It means that, despite your position (and your perception that you have a level of unconscious competence in what you do), there is something more you need to learn and that means, by definition, doing something that you might not feel confident about and so can fail at. This is to enter what I affectionately refer to as 'the belly of the dragon'; that place of uncertainty where who you are, what you do and how you do it are under question. No matter what senior leaders say, they rarely find this space easy or comfortable.

The absence of compassion for ourselves as leaders (and how we measure other leaders) is never so damning as it is in this space. Leaders, recognising they need to invest in their own education, avoid saying so publicly for fear of peer judgement. Vulnerability is not commonly seen as a leadership attribute (any more than compassion is) and to admit to the need to develop skills is to admit to a level of vulnerability that is challenging in front of other leaders and risky in terms of being on the receiving end of less than favourable judgment.

Yet, change is essential. What we now need in leaders is something more than what they know. Leaders have the capacity to change, but it must be safe for them to do so. They must learn to show each other (and themselves) compassion before they can show it to those they would lead. As is the nature of human revolution, however, the market is going to lead the change if leaders cannot lead it themselves.

The commercial case for compassion

The end result of the downsizing eighties and nineties, where loyalty and commitment were seen to be of no value, was the fomentation of the era of freedom of choice. There is now a new generation of young workers who rely on their own education and ability to secure their futures, offering and expecting loyalty from none.

The values of Generation X (roughly, those now aged between 25 and 40) were formed in the eighties and nineties. These are the children of the Boomers. Their parents worked hard, long hours and were the employees most on the receiving end of repetitious change. And their children witnessed it. The children saw their parents dedicate their lives to organisations and then have their efforts rewarded by lack of commitment and consequent loss of security. If their parents were able to create some degree of security for their retirement, it was because of their own efforts and shrewdness and not through the rewards of the organisations they variously worked for. The 'me' generation that the Boomers came to personify translated into a different sort of obsession with 'me and mine' for the Generation Xers. In fact, somewhat surprisingly, the values are inverted, despite both seemingly focusing on themselves.

The Boomers wanted (and respected) security, authority, rewards and recognition. They sacrificed much of their lives to their careers and to achieving or living by their values. Behind the scenes, many of their children then saw their parents' values thwarted (and had to deal with the fallout). They also grew up with split families and learned a level of autonomy that, contrary to popular myth that it brutalised them, they liked. In fact, they celebrated this independence. Generation X values emerged almost as an inversion of their parents' values. Today they want meaningful purpose, aligned values, choice, freedom to learn, a whole-of-life approach. They don't want to sell their souls to the company. They don't want a career at the expense of the rest of their lives (which encompasses family—however it is defined, sport, lifelong learning, travel and friends) and they definitely don't aspire to external security. In many ways, their needs in life sound achingly familiar (who wouldn't want these things, *if you could get them*). The difference is that they have the capacity to negotiate unswervingly for them with current leadership.

This is the commercial case for change. Smart leaders are now recognising that *creating and aligning people to purpose and values isn't a soft issue anymore*. It is now a crucial leadership skill. If you can't provide it, then you and your organisation will not be attractive to the very talent you will need to survive. If you don't know how to listen and to respond to what you hear, if you don't know how to give people a voice, to encourage learning at all levels, then Generation Xers will turn elsewhere.

While Generation X may be the first generation in a position to negotiate these outcomes in the average working environment, we all need them to prosper. Capacity can be built on these foundations. We learn and grow, feel safe in our learning and have a sense of inclusion. Leaders will help more people to achieve their potential when they lead with compassion, because what is good for the individual becomes what is good for the organisation, within reason.

This is also the commercial case for compassionate leadership—where the steward or custodian rises from the fray and accepts responsibility for measuring movement forward by something other than short-term profit.

Lessons not learned

I have witnessed so many stories to reinforce this in my journey, particularly in the last decade or so. In fact, while writing this chapter, an event happened which highlighted for me how reluctantly we learn the lessons of our time. A close friend of mine, a bright and engaging young man, was working in the advertising industry. He is a gentle and kindly individual who will, if invited, always go beyond the immediate request, always give more than is asked. He is also talented and creative. Most importantly, he is also 30—right at the heart of the Generation Xers. He rang me some time back to tell me that he had just been retrenched as a result of the last-on, first-off policy in his company.

My first reaction was anger, then hurt, then frustration. The advertising industry is not famous for the quality of its leadership. In fact, it has spawned a style of operating that ensures individual excellence is rewarded repeatedly over collective outcomes. (In the nineties in particular, paying hugely extravagant salaries to creative 'whiz kids' nearly brought the industry to its knees.) The industry has become opportunistic, with commitment to staff all too often tied to the latest client, rather than to a long-term objective or purpose. So, when a large client falls through, people are retrenched. The net effect is that smart young people negotiate high salary packages, have little if any loyalty, and change companies with alacrity, subject to the highest bid. This is not true of all companies in the field, but it is true of many and it demonstrates, better than many examples, the challenges of leadership in our times.

My friend had been in the job for 18 months when he was retrenched. After the first 48 hours, he had reconciled himself to the change and actually saw it as a positive. He has now made the choice to freelance and also to go back to school. He is living out the values of his generation by ensuring he has freedom and personal choice in his life. That's good for him and bad for the industry he has just stepped out of.

The organisation that once employed my friend made a short-term decision (based yet again on an opportunistic style of leadership) and as a result, in the future, when new clients come on board, they will find their human resource diminished or absent altogether.

There is also another hidden challenge in this scenario. Compassion is not just about how we treat people when we ask them to leave our organisations; it is about understanding the elemental impact on human community, on the climate of the business, as a result of doing this. How can we expect to engender commitment, loyalty and trust in our staff (of whatever generation) if we don't demonstrate it to them? Why should they give what they perceive leaders are unable to give?

We can say that this is the way the world is evolving (and many leadership writers have waxed lyrical about the extent to which the structure of future organisations will be based on satellite relationships and partnerships) but it is not what people want. My friend doesn't want to be in a relationship with people he doesn't trust or who don't show some allegiance to him in his life's journey. He will simply find it elsewhere, and in its absence, he will negotiate around money.

The balance between brain and heart

So, if this is the environment in which we operate, where does compassion fit and what is the role of compassionate leadership?

For individuals, compassion is the fine balance between brain and heart, between what we now call IQ and EQ (although it seems that these theories have hijacked what has been observable for eons in human behaviour). It is the difference between the long view (how to sustain an individual life as well as the collective) and the short view (how to ensure immediate gratification for a need such as food, material wealth and sensory experience). Both are important (as all who have survived in extreme environments know), but many of us nurture the one (the short view) at the expense of the other (the long view).

In essence, no-one wants pain or suffering and when we feel that it is our lot in life, we either exit from life or we speak out. To live with it is to accept a level of defeat that robs life of its joy. Ultimately, there is no one way to alleviate all human pain and suffering. It is part of our journey, existing in both the most affluent and the most needy of communities. But when it is a constant, *leaders beware*. The history of revolution is mirrored in this space.

Kindness, intelligence, human warmth and generosity are basic states we are all capable of demonstrating to ourselves and to each other. We all know that they kindle in our spirits a sense of worth that is far in excess of that which emanates from material success. In fact, external gratification is often sought because they are missing in our lives and food, entertainment and so on are easily accessed. We know, without being obsessive, that good friends, a loving touch, whispered warmth at a moment of risk taking, a friendly face in a crowd of strangers, and a helping hand in difficult times are worth their weight in gold (so to speak). We remember acts of compassion and kindness and are warmed by them long after the experience has passed.

That is not to say that material wealth doesn't matter—it does. It is fun, engaging, entertaining—easier to have it than not. Give a human being the choice between poverty and material comfort and you will quickly find out which they will choose (and in the process, we can acknowledge our predisposition to romanticise poverty and physical hardship!). Material wealth, however, is also the great seducer. It is good, but it is not enough, and to pursue it at the expense of a kinder way of living is actually to condemn ourselves to eternal dissatisfaction with what we have in life.

Profit as a measure of success feeds the existing paradigm and is about short-term thinking for self-gain and self-aggrandisement. By stark contrast, the triple bottom line (where profit and the economic measures of corporate performance are balanced by social and environmental parameters) is an act of compassion (and, ironically, in the long term, is commercially smart). As a framework for measuring our success, the triple bottom line helps us to ensure our decisions are responsible to the human community and to a sustainable environment. It also recognises that if we are not profitable, we are not able to achieve the social and environmental parameters, but to be profitable at the expense of the other two is to doom ourselves to a short and unhappy sojourn on this planet.

Compassion, founded on an understanding of human frailty and the importance of sustaining the long view, is demonstrated in adversity—in the application of beliefs, values and ethics when times are tough. It is easy to be nice when things are good. The test, however, is how we behave when what we know and want in life are at risk. Long-range, meaningful and constructive outcomes do not come from knee-jerk, short-term behaviour.

For many leaders, trapped in working environments where their experience is insufficient to the task, *the challenge is to balance an intuited sense of what is right with what makes for commercially good practice*. For such leaders, there appears to be an over-reliance on facts as a mechanism for making good decisions, as if facts (the component parts of the whole) are sufficient to describe the whole. They are not.

I have sat in on numerous senior executive discussions, which ebb and flow around a given announcement that must be made to staff but will be unpalatable to them. The leaders look at the facts, compile them, and then determine the format for their dissemination. Often in such meetings an individual will pipe up with: 'Bill is going to be upset by this', whereupon the other leaders will often respond with: 'Well, he'll just have to cope, there are more important issues to be dealt with.' These leaders are both right and wrong. On the one hand, there probably are other decisions to be made that, in the context of what has to be done, are more important or weighty from the leaders' perspective. However, what we consistently underestimate (because compassion is not a valued boardroom skill) is what it *feels* like to be on the receiving end of such a decision and, consequently, the impact (like a pebble in a pond) on the climate of the organisation.

Compassion is embodied in the act of giving and of giving generously (not in terms of donated good but in terms of thinking beyond self-gratification), especially when we are in a leadership role. Compassionate leadership invites us to think through the consequences of our actions and not just their content.

Leader, know thyself

As leaders, we must look at ourselves and our values and test how well we live them out. If we value affection, a sense of involvement, honesty, integrity, kindness, intelligence, purpose and learning in our own lives, how well do we afford them to others? What are our explanations for enhancing or diminishing such things in the lives of other people?

Being generous and compassionate with one another actually delivers more of what we want in life, makes us more capable, more valued as members of the human community. Being small-minded, money-driven, power-hungry and selfish might produce short-term results, but the end game is a risky one.

One of the great leadership researchers of our time was David McLelland, whose work on human motivation and the correlation between leadership performance and organisational climate is considered seminal. He made the observation that 30 per cent of organisational performance is climate related and 70 per cent of climate is determined by individual leadership behaviour. The filters that we, as leaders, use to understand the world before us and that then shape our behaviour profoundly affect what we consider to be 'right action'. In turn, that 'right action' shapes the climate within the organisation over which we have temporary captaincy. The question is: Are we influencing the climate naively, or do we genuinely understand ourselves, and then choose the most appropriate behaviour (the right action) subject to the people and situations we are leading?

In my experience, leaders need (now more than ever) to learn about themselves and their impact on the people around them. It is not enough to say 'all people are different'. We need to understand that difference and be able to lead accordingly.

For a wise leader, compassion is the driver behind personal flexibility—but personal flexibility cannot occur without first entering into a journey of self-enquiry. There is a wonderful little tool that I use to assist leaders to begin the journey of self-enquiry. It is called the JoHarri Map (it has been around for a long time and according to mythology was first developed by two people called Joe and Harry!). It's power lies in its simplicity (see figure 4.1).

Figure 4.1: The JoHarri Map

	Known by others	Not known by others
Known by self	**Public self**	**Private self**
Not known by self	**Blind spot**	**Potential**

The map is a great tool to help leaders understand the pragmatic value of a more compassionate style of leadership and helps them with a line of personal inquiry that may at first feel uncomfortable. The map helps leaders see that, irrespective of whether or not they want to reveal their vulnerabilities to others, those vulnerabilities will be apparent in their actions.

- In the top left-hand box, leaders are able to look at ways of behaving that they recognise in themselves and that others observe in them as well.

- The top right-hand box acknowledges the private part of our lives, known to ourselves but not open to public scrutiny.
- The bottom left-hand box, however, encourages leaders to be honest about what is *perceived* to be private but is actually seen by those around them. It helps them understand (through feedback from others) that, irrespective of whether you want it on show or not, your blind spot is understood and seen by others far better than it is understood by yourself.
- The bottom right-hand box acknowledges that continuous improvement is not a theory—it is an action and it starts with the capacity of leaders to self-reflect and develop. Potential is as relevant to the 60-year-old as it is to the six-year-old.

I believe leaders need to self-reflect as much as anyone else. Perhaps more so because of the impact their behaviour has— wittingly or unwittingly—on the people around them. Too often we entrench into 'terminal certainty', defending our opinions and our territory with the veracity of a lioness over the kill. In our passionate intensity we can overwhelm and silence difference and debate, and as we do this we lose a little—for ourselves, our families, our businesses and our communities.

In another life, I was national spokesperson (one of five international spokespeople) for the fur trade. I frequently found myself in artful, if not passionate, debate with people who found the fur industry vile and all who profited from it evil. Words were my stock in trade, so I could debate and often win with the best of the anti-fur lobbyists. Looking back, however, I am not proud of my actions. If truth be told, I agreed more often than I cared to admit with the other side of the debate. That is to say, I believe today (with some notable exceptions such as Siberia and Alaska!) that fur is an unnecessary luxury and that change in international practices was as inevitable as it was appropriate. At the time, however, I was effectively blind to entreaty. I think my family knew, however. They understood my values were at odds with where, through circumstance and naïve choice, I found myself. Eventually I was to face my own truths—expensively and publicly. Today I endeavour to help leaders do this before the consequences are as dire.

Conclusion

Compassion as a leadership virtue, then, is not something that can be objectified. It requires quiet self-reflection and a willingness to change as we learn. It is not about hard data or parts of a story, it is about wisdom and the capacity to look at the whole. It is also about understanding that games evolve over time, and with them the rules of success.

The times in which we live demand of leaders a level of insightfulness about their own behaviour that is possibly unprecedented in human evolution. We are not even sure that the concept of leadership as we now understand it will be sustained over time. Perhaps we will move from hierarchical structures (no matter how useful) to more intricate webs, based on relationships, in which leadership will ebb and flow with greater flexibility than our current structures permit.

This is a demanding time, then, to be in a leadership role. Having said this, we each have the potential to do the right thing by one another—and we know in our heart of hearts what that means. We know that acts of compassion are not 'soft' issues, as they have been so wantonly described so often by people who do not understand the intricacies of leading other people. We know that every time someone says: 'Look, we need to put the emotional stuff to one side and think this through logically and examine the facts', that something is fundamentally wrong with the statement.

We know that brilliant human minds can be used catastrophically for the worst as much as they can be used to enhance what we all need and want. We also know that transformation in our own actions takes time and determined focus, often in the privacy of our own lives as much as in a group setting.

In essence, compassion—for ourselves and for others—is our guide on this journey. It comes from confidence in who we are. It is about recognising that our actions, no matter how seemingly small, are significant. If all the challenges we face are the accumulation of thousands and thousands of actions, it is worth remembering that many of them were quite thought-less at the time. Our solutions may rely on the same process, namely thousands and thousands of small actions. Only this time, because we want it to be so, the actions may be thought full.

I wish it so, like everyone else on the planet.

Seven steps towards compassionate leadership

1 **Audit.** Audit your organisation and find out what people genuinely feel are the strengths and weaknesses of the organisation and its leadership. Find out what it is they believe you will not hear or change, and find out what they feel are the repercussions of this.

2 **Align.** Ensure purpose and values are clear and aligned, simple, passionately held, lived out and measured.

3 **Invest.** Invest in instruments for assessing leadership performance—360-degree appraisals, management style questionnaires and so on.

4 **Educate and support.** Only do step 3 if you are prepared to then invest in long-range leadership education and support. To ask people to lead, without providing them with the education and support that such a demanding role requires, is itself an utterly compassionless act.

5 **Assess and evaluate.** Then assess and evaluate leadership performance; measure it not just by the data but in terms of the stories that are told in the organisation by human beings.

6 **Seek feedback and reflect.** Don't think development is for everyone except you. If you are leading, you can be learning.

7 **Love a little, laugh a little, add a little.** Remember, 100 years from now almost every human being on the planet will be dead. Love people, make them smile, see what can be done to make the world a little kinder for your passage through. These gifts will be valued long after your passing, beyond money and fame.

For further exploration

—I recommend anything written by the Dalai Lama on the subject of compassion. This great human being has talked and written extensively on the nature of compassion. Although I am not a Buddhist, I believe his writings provide thoughtful, deeply loving and universally applicable insights into the nature of compassion. He also reminds us of the tenuous nature of our grasp on this mortal coil, of the unkindness of judgment, and of the importance of validating other human beings. These form the essence of compassion for me.

—Daniel Goleman, *Emotional Intelligence*, Bloomsbury Publishing, London, 1999.

Emotional intelligence has gained a great deal of attention in recent times. Truthfully, however, it is ancient. It is not about being sensitive and kindly, it is about being appropriate; understanding yourself and your impact on others, learning to do things differently (when, where and how different behaviour is appropriate), and understanding social settings and being behaviourally flexible accordingly. You can't and won't learn from this if compassion is not a guide. If it is, however, then this book will provide a wealth of interesting insights.

—Fabian Dattner, *Naked Truth: An Open Letter to the Australian Working Community*, Woodslane Press (now Allen & Unwin), 1996.

Between 1990 and 1995, I interviewed many thousands of working Australians. If you ever want a compelling reason to demonstrate compassion in leadership, borrow this from a library and read the countless stories (and the lessons I learned as a leader) from people in organisations who had been on the receiving end of thoughtless, inappropriate, disengaging, heartrending, stupid styles of leadership.

—Joseph Jaworski, *Synchronicity: The Inner Path Of Leadership*, Berrett-Koehler Publishers, USA, 1998.

This is potentially a little 'new age' and so might turn some people off, but pause a moment and read on. With an introduction by Peter Senge (of *Learning Organization* fame), this book provides a whole-of-life insight into the benefits of working with people for a shared vision and with aligned values. When this is done with good intent (some might say compassionate awareness), life has a way of delivering what you want and need as a leader. I have found this to be true and so, apparently, has Jaworski!

—Peter Block, *Stewardship*, Berrett-Koehler Publishers, USA, 1996.

An oldy, but a goody! This book (well researched and well written) reminds us of what leadership is all about: the art of the long view, acting on behalf of many over time, and not for a few in a short timeframe. I hold that stewardship is the product of compassionate leadership. As a steward, we are reminded to put our ego in our back pocket and think of the stakeholder community rather than our own achievements and rewards.

—Fabian Dattner, Jim Grant and Ken Luscombe, *Three Spirits of Leadership*, Business & Professional Publishing Pty Ltd (now Allen & Unwin), 1999.

This was written in collaboration with Jim Grant (my business partner) and Ken Luscombe, an eccentric Baptist minister who would hold any audience in his thrall. We each take a different voice—the voice of the entrepreneur (me), the corporation (Jim) and the community (Ken). We show that, through a compassionate filter, all three are needed in all places—the entrepreneur for the spirit of courage and risk-taking; the corporation for the spirit of good system and process; and community for the spirit of the long view, fighting for purpose bigger than self.

Note: Although I heartily recommend these books, reading is not really the path to compassion. That path lies with our children, parents, friends and fellow journeymen and women. Mostly, however, insight into compassion comes from how we feel about compassion when we are on the receiving end of it; that more than anything else is the great educator.

HUMOUR 5

Colin Benjamin

About the author

Colin Benjamin, MA (Political Science), BA (Economics and Psychology), Dip Soc Studies

Colin Benjamin is known to readers of AIM's *Management Today* magazine as Auntie Colin, the author of a regular column that throws brickbats and records bouquets from AIM readers.

Auntie Colin's alter ego is the Chief Executive Officer of *Life. Be in it.*™, an organisation he has been hanging around since before Norm was a gleam in Alec Stitt's eye. He is also the Managing Director of BEST (Business Expert Support Technologies).

Colin has been an Associate of the Mt Eliza Business School for more than a decade. Post-course evaluations show that his students are usually divided equally between those he has frustrated and infuriated and those who appreciate his habit of 'offering more one-liners than an episode of MASH'.

He is the creator of such business and management tools as the widely accepted Roy Morgan Values Segments and the recently released Privacy Pods© and ColourGrid©, which he uses in his management consulting practices The Horizons Network and Marshall Place Associates.

Colin is a Member of the Sun Tzu Research Society (Shenzhen, China). Having completed his earlier study at Melbourne University, he is currently working on a Doctorate of Business Administration at the Australian Graduate School of Entrepreneurship, Swinburne University.

Colin Benjamin can be reached at colbenj@lifebeinit.org.

Acknowledgment

This chapter could not have been written without the generous contribution and Internet research of one of Australia's brightest and most courageous young stand-up comedians, Adam Richard, and the acerbic editorial advice of Ms L Xuereb.

Introduction

Of all the virtues, humour is the most social and the most difficult to practise. Irony is infectious, sarcasm can be savage and satire satisfying, but humour takes daily practice and a lifetime commitment to communication with others.

Like Norm, the popular anti-hero from the *Life. Be in it.*™ campaign whom you will meet shortly, humour has to be exercised regularly and with due caution in order to make your life healthier and happier. Practice may not make perfect, but the benefit comes from actually doing it. As with so many aspects of life, it's the journey rather than the destination that counts.

Some people say humour is a gift from the gods; others confuse it with the gift of the gab. It's a necessity of life. In fact, at times it can be all that makes life bearable and its absence can be a source of boredom, depression and anger.

Humour functions like a trace element that is difficult to maintain in your diet. Without regular and sufficient doses of humour, the batteries that make life worth living are drained and become flat. Fun and games restock the larder of life for the bad and tough times that lie around the corner and offer the promise of happier times to come.

The overwhelming majority of us appreciate humour, enjoy it, share it and try to use it in difficult times. But what we find humorous varies from person to person and from moment to moment. It is cultural, situational and emotional. It can be elegant and witty or vulgar and base; cerebral or visceral; in your face or just beyond your grasp; uniquely personal or universal.

Various dictionaries define humour as:

The quality or condition of being amusing and funny . . . and . . . *the power to invoke laughter.*

To fully define humour would take more space than this chapter allows (and would be a most unhumorous exercise). When we try to analyse humour we impose a sort of false logic, we rationalise our own prejudice and reduce the fundamental elements to their lowest common denominator.

> *Analyzing humor is like dissecting a frog. Few people are interested and the frog dies from it.*
>
> EB White

So instead, let us examine the role and effect of humour in our lives, and its power as a leadership virtue.

The virtue of humour

So, why exactly should we accept humour as a 'virtue', a 'good thing' or even as something worth practising when conditions are less than perfect?

Whenever we exercise humour we find ourselves in touch with the other side of the exasperating realities that demand the presence of the calm, sane, considerate and thoughtful manager that we aspire to be. Unless we convert the negative energy associated with the turbulent, insane, ill-considered and careless actions of others into memorable relationships and 'better times to come', we enter a vicious cycle of aggressive and unfocused activity.

Only drawing down on our bank of life experiences gives us the insight and wisdom that encourages us to chuckle, smile or break down into tears of laughter when the impossible has just met the other side of coincidence. We know that the situation is absurd, unfair and intolerable, but it is now over and we can go on to enjoy the rest of our lives. That is one of the virtues of humour—*it allows us to manage our contextual reality.* When we are facing a stressful and intolerable situation, humour enables us to change our state of mind, to unwind, to reset the mechanism and then carry on.

When humour does more than just make us happy for a brief moment, but in fact helps us to find lifelong happiness, then to be humorous is indeed to be virtuous.

As managers we are constantly faced with complex problems, personal crises and impossible situations that in other circumstances might lead to crippling stress and anxiety. If we can stand back and give ourselves time to review our impulsive and immediate responses to stress, and if we avoid taking ourselves too seriously, we can prepare staff and colleagues (and ourselves) for the reality that life has to move on.

Humour, helping us to put life into perspective, enables us to keep going when the situation is so difficult or frustrating that we want to quit and find a life somewhere else. When it enables you to survive, to live and fight another day, then humour is truly a virtue.

The best medicine

Humour and laughter can literally be the best medicine. While it is legitimate to be sceptical of surveys, studies have found that hospital patients who experience laughter recover more rapidly than might be expected. Laughter appears to reduce heart disease, weight gain and depression.

Laughter and our responses to humour are known to release serotonin, one of the brain chemicals called endorphins, which stimulates emotional response. A lack of serotonin is the major cause of clinical depression, so drugs like Prozac and herbs like St. John's Wort are used to stimulate serotonin production. In times of adversity and stress the body balances our mood, reducing our levels of the stress hormone cortisol by giving us needed endorphins such as serotonin.

A US journalist decided to tackle a major debilitating disease by watching old Marx Brothers and Laurel and Hardy movie reruns. He and his physician found that 10 minutes of belly laughs gave him two hours of pain-free sleep and he went on to live an enjoyable pain-free retirement.

A clown is like an aspirin, only he works twice as fast.   Groucho Marx

---

An article in the *Sydney Morning Herald* (22 December 2001) reported that 'laughter has become a serious business'. Scientists have put it to the test and report that there is more to a hearty laugh than mirth and noise. A sustained belly laugh is good for blood pressure and heart rate, and there is evidence that it boosts immunity. All this research, done in the last 10 years, helps us understand the mind–body connection. A sense of humour allows us to perceive and appreciate the incongruities of life and provides moments of joy and delight.

In the face of adversity

We tap into patterns of meaning and the glass–half-full perspective when we 'laugh it off', 'share the joke' or see 'the funny side of it'. People who cannot exercise humour tend to put others down, have a joke only at others' expense and lose sight of the positive side of life.

Our ability to become efficient, effective and effulgent entrepreneurs and leaders depends heavily upon our capacity to distance ourselves from risk and uncertainty. We each have a vast array of fears, anxieties, worries and pressures. To succeed in life and business, we must develop coping mechanisms, such as humour, that allow us to move ahead with confidence, even in the face of fear and adversity.

As kids, we start life with a charged battery full of creativity, challenge and common sense. But as adults, do we still have the capacity for fun and enjoyment that comes from breaking all the rules, making a new path and setting the pace for others to follow? Why not? After all, wouldn't it be a force for change and the source of innovation and new business opportunities?

When the going gets tough, past and recent investment in fantasy, freedom and frolic provides the power to overcome obstacles, see other ways of tackling life's contingencies and re-establish a sense of balance and personal identity. This is the ultimate virtue of humour—it enables us to tackle life with greater confidence and commitment.

Humour and leadership

Try an interesting experiment. Go to your bookshelves or the AIM library, and take out a random selection of books on management and leadership. Now go to the index and try to find references to fun, humour and virtue. Don't hurry back. There are only a few brave souls who offer some reflections on humour. One is Robert Greenleaf who, when writing on the need to make life and business ethics an individual responsibility, makes the point that:

Purpose and laughter are the twins that must not separate. Each is empty without the other. Together they are the impregnable fortress of strength.

If I had the chance to rub Aladdin's lamp, one rub, one wish, I would wish for a world in which people laugh more. One can cultivate purpose to the point of having a glimpse of the ultimate and still remain connected with people and events, if one has humour, if one can laugh with all people at all stages of their journeys.

One of my current clients consciously measures the success and growth of his Japanese subsidiary company by incorporating fun into the key performance indicators of his entire leadership team. Even when selecting members of his top team, he is likely to turn up in a pink tutu and demand to know if the candidate knows how to be enthusiastic and enjoy herself. He will then introduce me as Norm's role model! This rapidly brings out the practical, personal and persuasive leadership side of the candidate, and separates those who would find it difficult to move beyond a managerial position.

This level of fun and enjoyment of working life helps to create rewarding relationships for all concerned (colleagues, customers and consumers) and contributes to their enjoyment of life and their living environments.·

The hierarchical barriers that create silos and sow suspicion in corporations tumble rapidly when the leadership team demonstrates that they are human, make mistakes and can learn from the comments and jibes of their colleagues. Customers enjoy working with sales team members who share the good times, have a good story to tell, are able to take part in pub sessions and can let their hair down. Consumers are willing to pay a little extra when they know that their service staff enjoy their work, pass on a good joke and clearly like working for a fun company that rewards their capacity to recover from emerging crises, unmet expectations and grumpy customers.

Leaders show that they care and can appreciate the stress and strain of deadlines, targets and under-resourced conditions when they muck in and muck up with their team members.

The virtue of leadership is often experienced in the mess, the aftermath of a mess and the mess of detail that are associated with good planning and attention to emergent and unpredictable conditions. Humour allows the team to find ways around the managerial constraints, the complaints from bureaucrats and other out-of-touch authorities. Humour helps relieve the tensions created by unreal demands for constant cost reductions and increased productivity, apparently without the presence of any human understanding, by line supervisors and project managers.

Whenever there are extreme conditions, tragedies, massive changes and other business conditions that lead to feelings of discrimination, depression and despair, it is the role of the leader to bring back a sense of perspective, uncover the funny side of the scene, rediscover the fundamental humanity of the team and encourage everyone to share the experiences.

Even under the most difficult of conditions, and particularly when there is crowding or isolation, humour has the virtue of releasing a shared sense of common values. This renewed sense of self provides a window of opportunity for compassion and consideration of the plight of others, and provides a space for the emergence of the other virtues that are the feature of sound leadership.

Jerold Apps comments that, in a society that seems to be increasingly pressured and focused on results, humour is sometimes sacrificed in the haste to get things done as efficiently as possible.

Rather than using up valuable time and seemingly diverting attention from the task at hand, humor serves many valuable purposes. First, and most fundamental, humor is a natural, human characteristic. We feel good when we laugh. We relax. Humor can surprise us, it can teach as well. An appropriate humorous story can make a point far more effectively than a dreary rundown of facts or details.

In 1975 the Hon. Brian Dixon, Minister for Youth, Sport and Recreation (more popularly known at the time as the Minister for Getting His Picture in the Paper), recognised the long-term health and education issues that were associated with the emerging TV society. Research showed that people were not prepared to spend 30 minutes a day on exercise and so it was critical to make fitness an associate of fun. The clear long-term vision was to get everyone to live more of their life and be more active, thus linking fun and enjoyment with long-term savings on heart/lung machines, hospital beds and the health system. Along with Alec Stitt, the creative genius behind Norm, and Philip Adams, the father of Australia's film and cultural revolution, 'Dicko' (as the Minister is still known around the world) generated nationwide support for the *Life. Be in it.*™ campaign.

This was the point where leadership met the bean counters. Could all state and federal governments overcome their political management perspectives to invest in a fitter, faster and more fun-filled nation? Was it possible to see beyond obesity, heart attacks and diabetes to fun runs, corporate cups, earth balls and a walk in the park?

Max Gillies and Philip Adams worked with Roland, Dorothy, Loraine, Stewie, Nev, Carol, Willy, Jenny, Darrilyn, Dot, Stella and Ian (and hundreds of others who deserve a mention) creating the most successful social marketing campaign that has survived the cuts of Treasury myopia for two decades. Norm sums up the whole story in this little poem:

Norm's Poem

Have you copped this bloke on the telly?
Interrupting me favourite show
With a tinny arranged on his belly,
Reminds me of someone I know.

Not that I'm against physical fitness,
Don't get me wrong on that score,
I could watch all them fit blokes forever,
But me thumb's inclined to get sore.

And I'm not against watching the telly,
Cripes if that was to go on the blink,
A bloke would have no sporting interests,
It certainly makes a bloke think.

Now it's true I might wheeze when I'm walking,
Not that I've done much of late.
And it's true I've put a few stone on,
But at my age you always gain weight.

So what if I can't tie me shoelace!
So what if I can't see me toes!
I remember what most of 'em look like,
So there's really no need to see those.

So when this bloke says 'Life. Be in it.'
Be in it, he says on TV,
I give him a nod and change channels,
'Cause I know he's not talking to me.

Case study: Norm and *Life. Be in it.*™

Nearly three decades ago, an unsuspecting public was introduced to the greatest Aussie anti-hero, Norm. Norm represents the slob in all of us, the couch potato we secretly enjoy being, and the character we think others should avoid becoming. Norm was the star of the *Life. Be in it.*™ campaign, which was a perfect example of humour as a leadership virtue.

Through the Norm campaign, advertisements for health and fitness education were dressed up as amusing cartoons that helped Australians overcome their denial of a fundamental reality: *self-delusion about our collective poor health was killing us.*

The purpose of the Norm campaign was to get Australians to change their habits of a lifetime, walk over and turn off the telly and be more active. This posed a major communications challenge because hostile audiences are resistant to receiving information, and the most resistant audiences are children (which is why our most successful educational programs feature puppets and cartoons and other amusing distractions to keep kids happy while they are surreptitiously educated).

Humour is a fantastic way of diffusing tension about life-threatening experiences. Fear often turns to laughter when we realise we have been afraid of something ordinary. You may have noticed often in films and television that high-anxiety moments incorporate jokes and humorous predicaments as a release valve, to siphon off some of the pressure. In life, too, this is a very useful tool. Laughter, or seeing the funny side of a situation, is a most effective way to prevent violent and other negative emotions rising to the surface, and to overcome fear of the unknown or change.

At *Life. Be in it.*™ we introduced *Life Games*, *Fit 'n Well* stadiums, *Dancing in Wheel Chairs*, and *There are No Excuses* programs. By doing so, we gave kids a parachute while they took risks and learned to enjoy team skills that encouraged them to be more active, quit smoking and see Australia.

Through the success of our campaigns, humour was shown to be an effective tool for improving the physical wellbeing of the entire nation. Subsequently, humour was used in a variety of other campaigns aimed at improving the mental and physical health of

Australians—campaigns such as *Find Thirty Minutes a Day* (diabetes), *Be More Active* (muscular dystrophy) and *Slip, Slop, Slap* (anti-cancer).

At the time of the Sydney Olympics, Aussie males achieved the second highest level of obesity (silver medal status) in the world and their kids were heading for gold as the fattest and most rapidly weight lifting 'fat-arsed wombats' in the history of Australia. So, Norm was forced to make a brief reappearance. On the occasion of his silver anniversary, he announced that he was coming out of retirement to 'go for Bronze' on behalf of Aussie males at the Athens Olympics.

Australians not only need to be more active, but also to recognise the vision and the leadership that was present two decades ago and to face the desperate need to revisit and revision our future at home, work and play.

A concerted effort is needed to ensure that Norm is well and truly out of medal contention by the time of the Beijing Olympics.

Humour in the workplace

Using humour as a tension release is especially effective in the workplace, where the inconsistencies and impracticalities of internal bureaucracy can cause frustration and anger. Looking at the absurd side of the coin can prevent you travelling down a darker, and more destructive, path. Take the following joke as an example of responses to an out-of-touch management situation.

The boss was doing his MBWA (management by walking around) routine and noticed a lad outside his office chatting with the receptionist. 'How much do you make a day,' he inquired. Told it was less than a *hundred dollars, he pulls out his wallet, gives the kid $100 and tells him to get out and don't waste his time any further. A few minutes later he rings reception to ask the name and job of the young bloke. 'Don't know,' he is told, 'but we can ring the DHL Couriers and find out, if you really want me to get him back'.*

That is why humour, as a leadership virtue, is so difficult to practise. It is exercised under the most trying conditions, is at its most effective when situations are tense, is appreciated when it resolves inherently confusing and contradictory experiences, and is savoured in darkened, smoke-filled rooms with a few survivors from the realities of life.

There are a number of paths to humour under difficult conditions:

- Comedy is an effective tool in education and information, assisting us in understanding issues and coping with potentially difficult situations.
- Satire diffuses apprehension and potential anger, showing us the absurdity of situations that could easily overwhelm us.
- Irony is a complex and distancing form of humour, which engages others in a revised perspective on an otherwise less than satisfactory situation.

One significant virtue of good humour is that it creates a positive view of life. It builds rapport and a common bond that can carry people through difficult times at the same time as making life worthwhile. As an element of management, it establishes the conditions under which people learn a living rather than just earn a living.

Managers who have a sense of humour create fun-filled workspaces, have high levels of productivity and don't need to dissect every situation to justify their fair share of paranoia and/or depression.

Laughter can lead to seduction, love and the carpet to the altar, whilst tears have the opposite effect. I have found that each of the above listed paths to humour contribute to my managers' toolbox.

If I can get you to laugh with me, you like me better, which makes you more open to my ideas.
                                                                John Cleese

In bad humour

Humour, like all tools, can sometimes be used as a destructive rather than constructive force. There are times when a joke will be taken the wrong way although, more often than not, the so-called joke in question was specifically intended to be hurtful or cruel. There are also times when levity can hinder rather than help a situation, distracting attention, pulling focus and slowing down a process.

The best humour comes from truth. When humour is used as a means to obfuscate facts or derail an intended course, it is coming from a place of negativity and falsehood.

One of the greatest skills of a comedian is to turn a potentially bad situation back into one of fun. People attend comedy performances to have a good time, in general, but there are always one or two people who are hoping to join in. Hecklers, however, do not have the audience's best interests in mind. They are looking to belittle the person on stage, in an effort to make themselves seem the funniest in the room. (Although, if you were to interview an audience, only the heckler's immediate friends are ever impressed with the outbursts.) This kind of humour is distracting and destructive, and it is one of the skills of a comedian to turn the situation around, repairing the rift between the performer and the audience. Comedians draw on what is known as the 'heckler comeback' or 'put-down', sacrificing that one member of the audience in order to save the group as a whole.

Similarly, leaders will sometimes be called upon to sanction instances of bad humour, and most often the best way is to fight fire with fire. Just as the comedian responds in kind to a heckler, it is sometimes necessary to prove that you can fight dirty. The occasional, and sometimes necessary, foray into negative humour will always reinforce the good humour that has gone before and that will no doubt surface again soon.

Leading and managing with humour

I would like to share a little of what I have learned about humour as a virtue during my time at *Life. Be in it.*™ We have a slogan, 'Every day is opening night', that suggests that life is not a rehearsal for something in the future but a new opportunity to change and improve our quality of life today. In endeavouring to live up to that slogan, my colleagues and I have gained leadership and management experience that we feel has made a significant contribution to the fun and enjoyment of our colleagues, customers and consumers (and to our own).

Live more of your life

I don't want to achieve immortality through my work. I want to achieve it through not dying.
Woody Allen

Norm has always enjoyed it when his sporting heroes go gold on his behalf—'Beaudy Newk', 'Goodonya Thorpie'. It is, however, costing millions of dollars each year to support fewer and fewer people to do a lot more to shave a few seconds off the personal best times of their sporting lives. *Life. Be in it.*™ believes we should *all* spend 30 minutes a day exercising to make sure that everyone can do a little bit more to improve their whole of life, rather than having a few do a lot for their brief sporting lives.

Some managers are helping Norm to achieve his goal of being out of medal contention for the Beijing Olympics by spending time with 'life coaches', taking time out to get to know their kids, investing in executive health and even taking time to have a real vacation— leaving the job behind and doing things with family and friends.

For more than a quarter of a century, we have been encouraging people to *Live more of your life*. It means that people add and restore value to their patterns of behaviour and find their spiritual centre in a materialist world. This needs to be reflected by our leaders in their policies and in how they spend their time and our money.

Life would be terribly boring if we did not take the time to do new things, make new friends and find those 30 minutes a day to get out and have fun.

Humour is a virtue whenever you can 'live more of your life'. As health educator Patty Wooten has pointed out so well:

Humour is a quality of perception that enables us to experience joy even when faced with adversity. Stress is an adverse condition during which we may experience tension or fatigue, feel unpleasant emotions, and sometimes develop a sense of hopelessness or futility.

Leisure and recreation are our lifesavers on the beach of life. They rescue us from the perils of over-work and over-serious, encouraging us to enjoy a happy hour and a long weekend. Find the opportunity to take time out, look to the long run and really enjoy those moments of fun with someone new.

Connecting with others

A country bloke decided he needed to go to the big smoke and meet a few new people. He got a job as a city courier and at the end of his first day his colleagues checked that everything was OK. The man responded that he had enjoyed a great day: 'Everywhere I went people asked for me autograph and told me where to go to see another of their old friends around town.'

It is interesting to note that the root of the word humour was the word for liquid or fluid—'umor'. Today, good humour can be released by sharing with friends a glass of the amber fluid or a glass of white. In modern dictionaries, humour is defined as 'a state of mind, mood, spirit'. Humour has the virtue of managing to reduce the social distance between us whilst increasing the links in our circle of friendships.

Life's a party where everyone is invited. You have to take yourself there and stop taking yourself seriously. A good party is a fun place to meet new people, have a good time and go home with a new friend. Getting involved with a new crowd of people ensures that you have the chance to talk about your needs, wants, hopes and expectations and then get out and do something about them with like-minded people.

We have found that people enjoy getting out and doing new things, going to new places and meeting the friends of friends. We have also found that managers can be so obsessed with their work and reputation that they are afraid to even talk to their colleagues.

Look for new friends by thinking outside the square. Break out of your corporate silos by converting every 'them' to one of 'us' as new friends.

The quickest way to release the tension in the workplace and avoid stressing out or struggling with problems alone is to take the first step and introduce yourself to new people. Finding out who is new in the zoo and laughing freely with others can be a powerful antidote to stress in the workplace.

Every time we lower the drawbridge on our castle of isolation and immunity, and contact people we haven't met before, we get the chance to expand our circle of old friends.

Forging companionships

You can get much further with a kind word and a gun than you can with a kind word alone.
Al Capone

Fellow workers are the most common source of new friendships. These companionships are often forged in the fire of fury, a shared sense of injustice and an un-unionised collective response to incompetent management. Look at lines such as: 'When I take a long time, I am slow . . . when the boss takes an impossibly long time, he's being thorough'; and 'When we do good, they never remember . . . when we stuff up, they never forget'. The only relief comes from the recognition that everyone is working for the same systematically poor excuse for management.

When we are faced with barriers, frustrating employers and resistant government bureaucrats, we often get angry, blame our colleagues or ourselves, or give up. If, however, we accept that each of the people we are dealing with believes that they are the victims of the same set of lunatic employers, we can share the stress we feel and lighten their load and ours without reaching for Al's gun.

Humour is the bubble pack that reduces the risk of breakage when someone or something in our work environment has once again failed to live up to our expectations. We can put up with a lot when we can laugh at our sense of the same insane conditions. In this way we can use humour as a signpost to the development of shared values and shared vision that permit us to campaign for better management.

Alignment

Working alone is a time losing equation; working with others is an opportunity cost; sharing good times makes up for lost time; but overtime can rapidly become boss's time and time to go.

Norm's view of working life

In the lexicon of any manager, there can be no doubt about the virtue of hard work. Norm has always believed in keeping it to the shortest possible duration, although he can watch others doing it for extended periods and with distinct pleasure. So, the key competence comes down to finding a way to make hours seem like minutes, weeks fly like days and years melt into memorable moments.

This magical mystery tour happens whenever we are able to convert associates into colleagues, friends into mates, and managers into visionary leaders. When shared values and shared vision are aligned with opportunities to work in small groups of like-minded individuals striving to overcome impossible barriers against even more impossible odds.

Under normal conditions, in the average organisation and with ordinary managers, there are always some dissatisfied employees who only do what they are asked to do. They fall into three categories: *clock-watchers*, *time-servers* and *troublemakers*.

The clock-watchers tend to feel isolated, have a life outside the gulag and are willing to do a fair day's work for a fair day's pay. Time-servers count back to the day that they are going to have a life in retirement doing all the things that they have worked for all their life. Troublemakers rely upon a group of mismanaged individuals who feel that their organisation has lost its way or does not recognise their potential to generate new and different perspectives.

Encouraging members of small groups to have fun, make a contribution and identify with the company's future not only benefits the team members, it can convert small pools of discontent into a river of revitalised opportunity.

Younger workers

An old blacksmith engaged in succession planning by taking on an apprentice from the village. He didn't like the idea much and showed it. 'Don't ask me a lot of questions,' he told the lad, 'Just do as I tell you'. A few days later, the old man took a red-hot iron out of the forge and laid it on the anvil. 'Get that hammer over there,' he said. 'When I nod my head, hit it real good and hard.' Now the town is looking for a new apprentice and a new blacksmith.

Humour has a special virtue when it encourages us to build an appreciation of the very different perspectives of younger workers (or, on the home front, family members). And yet, when we try to get managers engaged with their younger workers, they are quick to come up with excuses such as:

- They have to learn to look after themselves.
- I'm too busy at the moment to put up with their adolescent behaviour.
- It's easier to hire experienced workers than try to train young ones.
- I don't understand why young people today . . .

An investment in shared activities, pleasant times and good-natured banter, and finding time to listen to what younger workers find interesting and amusing, can develop a bank of good humour for the times when problems need to be addressed or behaviours modified. It also provides a culture in which learning can take place and the blacksmith's mistakes avoided.

Fun-filled workplaces are not only more productive, they also establish a positive learning environment, open the lines of access to management and create a breeding ground for competent, well-rounded professionals who act as role models for tomorrow's leaders.

Creating a future

If your parents never had children, chances are you won't either.

Dick Cavett

Creating a better future requires the ability to avoid taking the role of management too seriously and to instead taking on the mantle of leadership.

Leadership relies upon a combination of tolerance, patience, wisdom and generosity. These qualities can be in very short supply by the time that the very average senior executive arrives at the head of the queue for a short visit to the risible role of captain of a sinking ship. The average (too often, very average) chief executive is on the bridge for only a few short years.

Managers are best placed to win the support of their team and the mantle of leadership when they are able to share a joke, share the work and most importantly share the limelight when success arrives. Managers with a sense of humour are well placed to build a bridge to the future. Establishing happy hours, and even happier weeks, depends upon the capacity to see the funny side of things, and to create an atmosphere of fun, openness and enjoyment.

The virtue of humour lies in its permission to move beyond a culture of blame and finger pointing to giving space for reward and recognition of those who tackle tasks that are too big for them and who, more often than not, achieve the impossible.

In many ways, humour can be seen to be the glue that binds members of the corporate family to the goals and aspirations of the firm. There can be no progress, growth, or sense of achievement if there is no room for childish fun and games, no acceptance that accidents happen and that controlled mistakes have to be allowed to happen if there is to be an entrepreneurial environment.

Moving on

The manager is walking with his executive coach, who happens to be an economist. 'Thank you,' he says. 'I now understand the jargon you guys go on with . . . your hair is in recession, your tummy is a victim of inflation and, taken together, they are leading us both into depression.'

Our experience with social marketing campaigns has taught us to keep the message simple, repeat it often and, most importantly, provide many opportunities for people to actually enjoy taking part in the process of change. Humour can help 'the boss' to make the changes that others might find difficult to accept and help all concerned to cope. (This is, of course, preferable to a demeaning personal and public loss of face that serves to focus anger upon defensive behaviour and readily mobilises a mutiny in the office.)

A smile and positive atmosphere communicate that management is not hostile and they can make unpleasant truths palatable, soften the blow in hard times and encourage acceptance that, as the old proverb goes, 'Many a true word is spoken in jest.'

Humour has the virtue of momentarily releasing tension and feelings of anger and fear, while offering a window of opportunity to once again feel carefree, light-hearted and hopeful. Learning to laugh is the catalyst that releases the hidden talents and spirit of life that underpin any business, and allows us to accept change and move on.

Some people can see auras that others cannot experience without access to Kirlian photography, while the application of the healing touch of someone who cares can bring relief. Humour also heals. We can all get back in touch with our vital essence, the cradle of the Spirit of Life, whenever we accept the forces of fate and learn to laugh.

We need to step out of our sensitive comfort zone and release past failure. Guided by our Spirit of Life we take only the positives from the past and dream, envision and create a better future. When we share our plans for a lottery win or a big win at the Melbourne Cup, we bring others into our world of hope and encourage others to work towards common goals.

Conclusion

Laughing at yourself is not always easy. Frequently one is too immersed in a problem to find any humour in it. It can help to seek out people with that special flair for seeing the funny side of a situation; to use the talent available to aid in the quest for laughter and comic release.

Patty Wooten

Humour is a virtue whenever you want to *Live more of your life*, meet people who have different values and life experiences, and take the time to touch other people's lives long enough for them to make the journey from associates and colleagues to lifelong friends.

The best way to make sure that kids are on the right track is to give them the freedom of association with a better class of life experiences, add diversity to their range of experiences and give them a better choice of parents at the time of their birth. *Prejudice* and *ignorance* are BBQ mates—they meet in redneck kitchens and are either overdone or underdone expressions of parents' failure to provide a requisite variety of experiences for their children.

Hard work and a hard life are only an excuse for misery when the ability to laugh, share good and bad times, and enjoy a walk in the park have been replaced by the handicap of carrying around the idiot in your own shoes. Finding the time for leisure and recreation is a sure-fire way to put back the missing fun in your life and to discover the future that nearly took the wrong turning and passed you by.

The many jokes about bosses, computers and office parties attest to the fact that many workplaces could do with an injection of *Fit 'n Well at Work*. Humour has the virtue of reprogramming the world of work into confined spaces between the commercial pressures and time with family and friends.

We need to remember that our boy Norm is an anti-hero, not a role model. It's a real problem when we have to bring him back to offer some leadership and get us to find the funny side of ourselves; to get our kids to give up their Gameboy and Xbox and 'turn off the telly'.

Leadership is an individual responsibility that grows out of self-awareness, a sense of purpose and the commitment to a sustainable future. We can use humour in our daily lives to distance ourselves from business pressures, world wars and global warming but, in the end, we must make a virtue of self-awareness and social responsibility.

The ultimate virtue of humour for leaders and business arises from the richness and diversity of succeeding and successful generations of self-directed, fun-loving and productive lives.

Seven lessons for leading with humour

1 To 'Live more of your life' involves time with others.
2 The more new people you meet, the more old friends you make.
3 Trust and trouble are companions on the path to true friendship.
4 Hard work is only fun in small groups for short periods of time.
5 Engaging with young workers creates a future for us all.
6 It's easier to hang on to the past than hang out for the future.
7 Learning to laugh helps leaders and followers to cope with change and difficult times.

For further exploration

The ultimate texts on humour and business are the works of *Dilbert* and Don Scott—nothing more needs to be read. But if you have a serious desire to look at leadership, consider:

—John Adair, *Effective Leadership*, Gower, Aldershot, UK, 1983.
Adair provides a clear explanation of the special set of relationships that develop effective leadership, including the critical role of humour as a form of glue that binds together the rings of leadership.

—Jerold Apps, *Leadership for the Emerging Age*, Jossey-Bass, UK, 1994.
Apps takes a modern, integrative approach to leadership and looks to humour as an element of successful leadership processes for the twenty–first century.

—Robert Greenleaf, cited in MS Peck & PR Senge, *Reflections on Leadership*, John Wiley & Sons, New York, 1995.

Greenleaf offers a comprehensive, person-centric (rather than organisation-centric) approach to leadership, advocating that leadership should be thought of as a way of life rather than just as a business function.

—Craig R Hickman, *Mind of a Manager Soul of a Leader*, John Wiley & Sons, New York, 1990.

Hickman provides an excellent range of models of management and leadership, plus a Myer–Briggs type instrument to enable readers to identify their own place in the management–leadership hierarchy.

PASSION

6

Charles Kovess

About the author

Charles B. Kovess, LL.B (Hons), LLM, CSP, MAICD, MAITD

Charles Kovess is the founder and Managing Director of Passionate Performance, and is known as 'Australia's Passion Provocateur'.

After practising law successfully for 20 years, Charles left that profession in 1993 to pursue his passion for increasing passion! Today, Charles assists organisations around Australia to harness the power of passionate performance. Clients include Deakin Australia, ANZ Banking Group, Tourism Victoria, Commonwealth Bank of Australia, National Australia Bank, Optus, Essendon Football Club, Knight Frank, Brisbane Lions Football Club, Telstra, Axa (formerly National Mutual), the Federal Department of Finance and Administration, the Victorian Department of Treasury and Finance, Australia Post, Colonial State Bank and Uncle Ben's.

In March 2001, he earned the coveted 'Certified Speaking Professional' accreditation—the highest qualification internationally for speaking professionals.

Charles divides his spare time between writing, sport (he is a triathlete) and voluntary activities. He is President of the Australia–Hungary Chamber of Commerce (for the eleventh year), President of the Global Energy Network Institute and National Vice-President of the National Speakers' Association of Australia.

His first book, *Passionate People Produce,* was released in 1997 and became a bestseller. His second book, *Passionate Performance,* was released in 2000.

Charles Kovess can be reached at charles@kovess.com or at www.kovess.com.

Introduction

It's time to be clear about, and committed to, the *spiritual dimensions* of business and leadership and the role of passion as a leadership virtue.

Since 1993, in my role as 'Australia's Passion Provocateur', I have been promoting the power of passion. It's been a tough road. Life would have been much more financially rewarding if I had stayed in my original profession of law. But I gave away a large and predictable income as partner in a successful law firm because of my passionate belief that Australia's future is totally dependent upon the quality and behaviour of our leaders, in all fields of endeavour.

If my four children, and your children, are to inherit an Australia that is sustainable, successful, enjoyable and full of possibility, then what is required is *leadership with a spiritual dimension*—and at the moment that is far too uncommon. My exposure to many hundreds of Australian organisations though my work has shown me that only a minority of our executives are willing to engage with this dimension of the organisations that they lead.

The 'spiritual dimension' of business is the part of business that is not of physical or mental dimensions. It encompasses culture, caring, inspiration, team spirit, fun, virtuousness, ethical and moral behaviour, courage, integrity and, dare I say it, love!

And what is the key to unlocking the spiritual dimension of leadership? The answer is *passion*.

In this chapter, I will share the ideas about passion (and the strategies to promote it) that have driven and guided me for the 50 years of my life; and that I have shared with many people in many companies. These ideas can make a significant and positive difference. Leaders of large and small organisations have successfully implemented them. So can you!

The ideas shared in this chapter are *simple, but not easy*. This is an important dichotomy. There is a very strong temptation to discard good ideas because they are difficult or will take time to implement—hence the many management and self-help books whose titles promise easy solutions . . . a limited number of steps to success . . . the answer lies within the covers . . . leadership isn't hard . . . all you need are the secrets of the author (and so on).

Examples of the simple/easy dichotomy include: it is a simple process to get physically fit (just walk four times a week for 30 minutes each time), but it is not easy; it is a simple process to lose weight (eat less), but it is not easy; it is a simple process to avoid addiction to work (spend more time with your loved ones), but it is not easy.

Here is another paradox. When we do the hard things, our lives become easy. Conversely, if we look for the easy ways, our lives can become very hard! For example: when we train hard to get fit, it is easier to handle life's challenges; when we study hard to gain outstanding academic results, life becomes easier because we can get a job more easily; when young people take it easy by using drugs, and they become addicted to them, their lives become very hard.

So, I encourage you to see beyond the easy fix. When it comes to passionate leadership, I don't have a passion pill that will do all the work for you. I am certain, however, that if you apply these simple concepts your leadership skills and effectiveness will become a source of great fulfilment for you.

What is passion?

My personal definition:

Passion is a source of unlimited energy from your soul (or spirit or heart) that enables you to produce extraordinary results.

Why an *unlimited* source of energy? In my own life I have found that, when I am passionate about something, I seem to be able to tap into an unlimited source of energy. I don't become tired and seem to able to go on and on until I achieve what I am seeking.

Why *extraordinary*? What most people generate is 'ordinary', whilst passionate people go beyond the ordinary!

I found the following quotation on a *Successories* card in a bookshop. I have not been able to track down the author (please let me know if you have), but it encapsulates my thoughts on passion:

Passion is powerful . . . nothing was ever achieved without it, and nothing can take its place. No matter what you face in life, if your passion is great enough, you will find the strength to succeed. Without passion, life has no meaning. So put your heart, mind, and soul into even your smallest acts . . . this is the essence of passion. This is the secret to life.

Author unknown

I love the word 'passion', but others prefer words such as 'enthusiasm', 'inspiration', 'energy', 'motivation' or 'desire'. Each of us has learned to interpret words to mean certain things, particularly under the influence of our family and community environments, so some people prefer to avoid using 'passion' because of negative connotations.

Passion can be linked to any activity whatsoever, be it ever so grand, or ever so minor. The attention to detail of a passionate stamp collector is no less worthy than the passion of a world–class sportsperson. In my first job in a solicitor's office in 1969, I discovered how important the (seemingly) mundane tasks could be. If a letter of demand was not posted on a particular day, and appropriate record kept of the day of posting, the legal ramifications could have been devastating. Every organisation needs people who are passionate about the 'big' things and the 'small' things.

So, just as leadership can exist at many levels of the organisation, regardless of explicit or formal titles, so too can passion. Permission is not needed (although, for reasons to be discussed later, it can be challenging to be passionate when most others are not).

It is important to realise that each person demonstrates passion in his or her unique way; there is no right or wrong way to be passionate. Don't fall into the trap of judging another person's passion levels according to the way that you exhibit passion, or by the Hollywood stereotypes of passion (loud, extroverted, emotional or choleric). There are overtly passionate people, but there are also quiet, humble, introverted people whose lives are driven by passion.

As each of us demonstrates passion uniquely, I won't be prescriptive in my description of it. There are some clues, however, that signify the presence of passion. In the workplace they include:

- unlimited energy for the task at hand
- persistence in creating an outstanding result
- willingness to challenge others who attempt to demean or belittle the task
- willingness to take responsibility or accountability
- willingness to speak the truth about the task (particularly when a person chooses to be a 'whistle-blower').

Passion is the key to successful leadership because *it engages more than the mind*. As stated earlier, passion is a source of unlimited energy from the heart (or soul) that enables a person to produce extraordinary results. It is passion that gives us our purpose and direction. Our minds, on the other hand, are designed to help us to pursue that purpose.

Why aren't we more passionate?

As a professional speaker, I spend a lot of time in front of many different audiences. I ask each of these audiences: 'How often are you impressed by the passion of the people who serve you in large national department stores or in Australia's banks?' And invariably there is spontaneous laughter! It is a very rare event indeed for customers of such large institutions to experience service from a passionate staff member. Often the comment that follows is that just finding someone to serve you can be difficult!

I have asked these audiences to 'guesstimate' how many people are passionate about their work, and some 80 per cent of respondents say that less than 20 per cent of our workforce impress them as being passionate. This anecdotal evidence is persuasive, and I believe it is close to the truth, regardless of the exact definition of passion that each person may use.

And yet, I cannot remember speaking to a person who was not genuinely excited, enthusiastic, indeed passionate, about starting a new job. What happens to this excitement, enthusiasm and passion? I believe that it is the quality of leadership that is a fundamental factor in destroying new employees' passion—and leaders who do not understand this are damaging the futures of our organisations. In this context, 'leaders' includes the managers to whom employees report.

Over the past two decades, there has been increasing pressure on corporations to generate quickly ever-increasing returns on capital and this has meant a correlating focus on economic rationalist philosophies. This has led to a corporate mindset that business has no other responsibility than to make profits, and that employees are a cost rather than an asset. I believe this pressure has largely destroyed employee loyalty as well as passion. It has also ensured that emotions don't have a place in the leader's toolbox.

Some leaders have good reason to fear passion. Their life experiences have taught them the dangers of passion at the expense of reason and logic. After all, the unbalanced pursuit of passion (or any virtue for that matter) can create great trauma and harm. So these leaders have made a sensible decision to restrain and control their passions.

Alternatively, a leader may have had previous bad experiences with passionate employees, whose energy and purpose was not aligned with that of the organisation (more of this later).

Another factor is that many organisational leaders have been promoted from the ranks of the more rational fields of engineering, accountancy and law. Feelings and emotions sit uncomfortably amongst such influences . . . fearing passion makes sense.

Kahlil Gibran, in *The Prophet*, explores the dichotomy between passion and reason:

Your soul is oftentimes a battlefield, upon which your reason and your judgment wage war against your passion and your appetite . . .

Your reason and your passion are the rudder and the sails of your seafaring soul.

If either your sails or your rudder be broken, you can but toss and drift, or else be held at a standstill in mid-seas.

For reason, ruling alone, is a force confining; and passion, unattended, is a flame that burns to its own destruction.

Gibran then goes on to acknowledge the importance and relevance of both reason and passion. He equates them to two guests in our houses, and asks us not to favour either.

The purpose of my work revolves around understanding and accessing passion, without favouring it at the expense of reason; balance between the two is vital.

Now is the time for passion

Business is operating today in a fluid, volatile, changing and globalised environment. Competition is fierce and timeframes are shortening. Strategies that have succeeded over the past decade (such as downsizing, outsourcing, cost-cutting) are no longer available. New strategies are required in this Knowledge Age.

Beyond the short term

Leaders are often seduced by short-term thinking, at the expense of thinking and caring about the long-term, sustainable performance of their organisations. Consider the correlation between the corporate disasters of Enron, Andersen and WorldCom, and the ban on performance-enhancing drugs for sporting competitions.

- Short-term hunger and desire to generate profits, at the expense of integrity, truth, people, ethics, morals and principles, lies behind these corporate disasters.
- Short-term hunger and desire to win a competition lies behind the choice to take illegal performance-enhancing drugs.

How can you create any performance of substance without 'doing the work'?

- Tiger Woods did not become the best golfer in the world with short-term thinking!
- Nelson Mandela did not become an inspirational leader and influencer with short-term thinking!
- Turkey did not achieve its third place in the 2002 Football World Cup with short-term thinking!
- Dr Graham Clark did not invent the bionic ear with short-term thinking!

So, isn't it about time that the pressure—by 'unthinking' short-term institutional investors—to think in the short term in order to generate ever-increasing corporate profits is discredited? It's a lousy way to build a business! And we should be suspicious of any corporation that grows much faster than its competitors, as recent corporate disasters now reveal.

Some of Australia's most-respected business writers are expressing similar views. On 29 June 2002, in the *Age*, Stephen Bartholomeusz wrote:

Executives who could deliver consistent increases in earnings were able to benefit themselves (through stock options) and fund managers (through attracting more funds to be managed). That alignment had little to do with the long-term interests of companies or investors. What it encouraged was greed, recklessness, and fraud. Everyone won when 'the numbers' kept rising, whether or not those numbers were real.

And in the *Australian Financial Review* on the same day, Alan Kohler wrote:

WorldCom has also highlighted the dangers of share-based payments to executives. While they turn managers into owners . . . there remain differences in the way each of them experiences ownership, which undermines the aim of the idea. Specifically, management share options come with no cost and no risk, and managers also have a far shorter time-horizon than shareholders saving for retirement.

Here are some helpful strategies for overcoming short-term thinking:
1. Decide to become passionate about your organisation's long-term future.
2. Learn the purpose, vision and values of your organisation, word for word, just like your maths tables, so that you know when steps are being taken that are inconsistent with these three key concepts.
3. Decide what your own morals and ethics are, and then act according to them—regardless of the financial implications—whether you are at work or elsewhere.
4. Speak more of the truth, as you perceive it. It doesn't matter whether you are 'right' or 'wrong'—the point is that you express your views.
5. Access your courage to be different, to be true to who you are, rather than following the crowd because it is safer to do so.

Courage is the most important capability of high-performance leaders.

6. Make some long-term decisions yourself, such as deciding to lose weight, or get fit—and stick to them. In Australia, 65 per cent of men are 'fat or obese'. How can a nation succeed when such large numbers of people refuse to take care of themselves for the long term?

7. Persist! Stop looking for short-term results.

People power

The key to ongoing and sustainable business productivity is to access the creativity, innovation, entrepreneurial spirit and energy of the most important asset of every business—its employees. In today's challenging environment, business success hinges on the knowledge of employees and, unfortunately, that knowledge can walk out the door at any time.

Employees will perform at optimal level when they *want* to. And unless they want to, they will not perform at the level of their true potential. Passion is a key component in creating the *want* or *desire*. An attitude that embraces change, that loves change and challenge, is now a strategic resource.

Since the early nineties, loyalty from larger employers towards their employees has largely diminished, and so has the concept of a career for life in the one organisation. Employees have learned the hard way that they need to look after themselves, so their loyalty is naturally much reduced. They are open to the next bidder, and retaining top talent is becoming one of the key challenges that leaders must meet.

Every employee has different motivators, and leaders who don't understand this will not generate above-average profits. This is because the profitability of an organisation is directly linked to the energy of the people within the organisation and, in particular, to the energy of the leadership team. What is the link between energy and profits? It is that money is essentially a representation of human energy. The equation can be expressed like this:

- Human beings bartered goods and services.
- Money was invented to replace barter.

- Goods and services were the direct result of human beings 'doing things'.
- The more things they did, the more they could barter.
- The amount of human energy determined how much could be done (that is, each person's productivity).
- Thus, the more energy you had, the wealthier you would become.

This equation is still relevant. The productivity of a leader and other employees is directly linked to energy. Leaders must increase the energy within all employees by leading with passion, and by encouraging others to be passionately engaged in their pursuits.

Getting emotional

I believe that caring for employees is a critically important factor in business success, and unless employees feel their employer cares about them, their initial passion for their jobs fades too easily. Caring is an *emotional* process.

Daniel Goleman's book *Emotional Intelligence* (or 'EQ') struck a powerful chord when first published in the mid-nineties and interest in the field, as shown by business articles and publications, is not waning. Emotions are the key to motivation, and motivation starts with people *wanting to act*. This desire is a powerful fuel for performance.

In *The Human Equation* by Jeffrey Pfeffer, Sam Walton (of Wal-Mart fame) is quoted as saying that the key to his extraordinary success was to understand this rule:

The way management treats employees is exactly how the employees will treat the customers. And if the employees treat the customers well, the customers will return again and again, and that's where the real profit lies, not in trying to drag strangers into your stores for one-time purchases.

So, when employees feel cared for by their employers, their performance improves.

The power of passionate leadership

Accessing passion as a source of energy will make you a powerful, confident, secure and inspirational leader. It will change your life, and change the future track of your organisation. Let me demonstrate the power of passion by listing the negative consequences of a dispassionate leader and environment:

- The leader has low personal energy.
- The organisation isn't vibrant, revolutionary, growing or exciting.
- Creativity and innovation are resisted, indeed punished, particularly when things go wrong.
- The organisation is driven by a culture of fear and avoidance of risk, rather than by one of growth, expansion and possibility.
- Behaviours that are ethically and morally questionable are exhibited and condoned.
- Telling the truth is seen as dangerous.
- There is a general tendency to avoid responsibility and accountability.
- The employees' level of respect for the leader is low.
- Employees feel that the organisation doesn't care about them.
- Levels of fun are low.
- Stress levels are high amongst employees.
- Staff turnover is high.

Energy

Currently, many of the top 1000 companies are losing, or disposing of, their CEOs at an alarming rate. Why? Because many CEOs have simply lost their drive and energy. Boards dump them because they are worn out! These tired CEOs don't have the energy to fight for their visions of the future, or to reinvent themselves and their management teams to cope with and conquer new or changing business conditions.

Passion provides CEOs with the energy they need to constantly and consistently exercise creativity and vision, and to cope with the fast and unremitting pace of life at the top. So, the lesson to be learned is clear. All leaders must access their passion and jealously guard their energy sources, particularly by creating a balance of mental, physical and spiritual elements in their lives.

Inspiration and engagement

Successful leaders understand the need to appeal to employee motivators that are more important than next week's pay cheque. Inspiration and motivation occur on a long-term, sustainable basis when the achievement of business goals is aligned with the purpose and the goals of employees.

When you are inspired by some great purpose, some extraordinary project, all your thoughts break their bonds. Your mind transcends limitations, your consciousness expands in every direction, and you find yourself in a new, great and wonderful world. Dormant forces, faculties and talents become alive and you discover yourself to be a greater person by far than you ever dreamed yourself to be. Patanjali

---

When did you last discover yourself 'to be a greater person by far than you ever dreamed yourself to be'? Have you ever truly been inspired by some great cause, some great project? Inspiration is a spiritual matter, and being inspired is a wonderful way to live life. What would happen in your business or organisation if most of the employees were inspired about their roles and their work?

Your business has a higher purpose (or mission) than just making a profit. Making a profit for shareholders does not inspire employees for the long term. The higher the purpose that a leader can find, the more willing employees will be to engage their minds as well as their hearts and souls. If your business purpose is solely to make a profit, many in your team will refuse to commit all that they can, and will simply do their jobs for their salaries, without inspiration. As a leader, you will be left yearning for more, and wondering 'why is it so difficult to find good employees these days?'

Arie de Geus, in *The Living Company*, eloquently described the difference between profits and purpose with this beautiful metaphor:

Profits for business are like oxygen to human beings; they are essential for survival, but they are not the purpose.

It is the role of the leader to clarify the purpose of the organisation, and to put it in such terms that employees are inspired. Of course, if the leader is not passionate, this becomes an almost Herculean task.

Let us consider Telstra Corporation in Australia, one of the largest and most profitable businesses in the country. Does Telstra have a higher purpose than just to generate profits? I believe it does. One example of Telstra's higher purpose might be to *facilitate communication between human beings*. A higher purpose still could be to *promote tolerance and harmony between people through improved communication*. What a stunning higher purpose that would be!

The ANZ Banking Group offers another example of higher purpose. For some years, I have facilitated programs with groups of ANZ employees as part of their leadership development. I once asked these future leaders to describe the purpose of the bank. Most of them said that it was 'to make money'. Upon detailed discussion, all of them agreed that a far more inspirational purpose revolved around the customers of the bank. I invited these future leaders to consider the original founders of the ANZ Bank and their thinking and motivation when they established the organisation. They then described the inspirational purpose of the bank in the following terms:

The purpose of the ANZ Bank is to solve our customers' financial and banking needs through the passionate performance of our people, in a way that delights those customers.

The reason such a purpose statement can inspire is clear—it revolves around people! Relationships impact on our souls, our spirits and our hearts. Money is less likely to do so. If money is the purpose, then a focus on results and benefits to customers and clients is difficult. Promoting 'money' as the purpose means that every employee is constantly and solely focused on extracting money and fees from customers and minimising expenses, rather than serving the customers and adding value to their lives.

In the words of my friend David J Wood, in his unpublished poem:

Does your organisation's purpose
Excite and inspire,
Or does it require,

All words of desire
To shrink and retire,
So the 'gurus' can fire
Their language most dire,
With words that require
All employees' desire,
To depart or retire—
So that profits can grow?

It is possible to frame any organisation's purpose statement around the value that the organisation gives to human beings. Leaders who do this, and then passionately commit to the purpose, will discover the extraordinary impact that inspiration, and spiritual elements, can have on the performance of the people that they lead.

Leaders who wish to influence and inspire other people are more likely to succeed in the long term when they are passionate and inspired by the purpose they are pursuing. Unlimited supplies of energy become available; those who come into direct contact with such leaders are struck by their presence, confidence, strength and believability.

If a leader is convinced an idea or strategy is going to succeed, then he or she will be able to influence and inspire both the Board of Directors and those who are led to commit to the cause. The alternative scenario is obvious.

Courage

The word 'courage' derives from the Latin word 'cor' meaning 'heart'. In fact, it is when we follow our heart that we are truly being courageous.

Our minds are designed to protect us, and often our minds are in conflict with our hearts. A classic example of this is a soldier at war. When he is fired at, his mind says: 'Run!' His heart, however, says: 'I'm fighting for my country, so I won't run.' That is courage. It is not the absence of fear but, rather, it is acting despite fear.

A leader cannot be guided by fear. That is not inspirational and empowering in these tough and fast-changing times. The trouble is that our minds can easily be dominated by fear.

Walt Disney was an extraordinary, passionate visionary. He refused to allow his company to be driven by short-term share price demands. He had the courage to follow his heart and overcome the fear his mind kept raising—lack of money. In Bob Thomas's authorised biography of Disney, the point was clearly made:

When the stock was in a slump during the post war period, influential stockholders urged the Disneys (Walt and his brother Roy) to announce a big expansion in order to inflate the stock price. The threat of stockholder suits was raised. The Disney answer: 'Sue all you want. We're doing what we think we should do, and that's to take care of the best interests of the company, not any individual stockholder.'

It takes courage to behave contrary to 'conventional wisdom'. Yet how can an organisation generate above-average returns if it behaves in an average way? Here is an example. What do you think is the relative importance to business success of employees, customers and shareholders? In what order of importance do you believe they should be ranked to create outstanding, sustainable results?

Conventional wisdom ranks them in this order:
1. Shareholders   2. Customers   3. Employees

Successful leaders, such as Richard Branson and Sam Walton (as reported by Jeffrey Pfeffer in *The Human Equation*) say that the relative importance is:
1. Employees   2. Customers   3. Shareholders

To act in this way, however—putting employees first—requires courage because you must challenge conventional wisdom. If you are passionate about generating above-average returns, you will have the requisite courage.

So, let's en-*courage* our leaders to be passionate, to be true to themselves, and to become real leaders. That's the way to build a great organisation, and many great organisations can build a growing Australia, a successful Australia, a balanced Australia, where we have soul, as well as cash, and an outstanding national future!

Responsibility

The mark of a true leader, at whatever level, and whether formally nominated or not, is *willingness to take responsibility*. Leon Gettler's recent article in the *Age* discussed the findings of an Australia-wide survey of almost 30 000 people (conducted by Human Synergistics in 2002). The survey revealed that an overwhelming majority of leaders and managers are driven by fear, a desire to avoid risk and a desire to avoid taking personal responsibility.

My passionately held belief is this: the leader and each and every employee in every organisation is personally responsible for the success of that organisation and, ultimately, for the long-term success of Australia. We cannot afford to keep passing the blame to others.

Twenty years' experience as a tax lawyer showed me that we live in an 'analgesic society'. If something goes wrong, or some money is lost, find someone or something to blame. Find the 'analgesic pill' of a remedy against another. Relieve the problem with a court case or a refusal to pay money, but do not, in any circumstances, acknowledge that the problem might lie with you—or that you are actually responsible. Find a reason to justify what you did, so that the fault cannot be said to lie with you!

In organisations it is so easy to blame others, to justify a situation because of someone else's behaviour, or to 'pass the buck'—because we convince ourselves that we don't have the relevant position or authority to do something about the situation. Taking responsibility for our lives, for our organisation's and for our nation's future can be difficult, terrifying and dangerous. And yet, at the same time, it can be liberating, energising and motivating.

Life is either a daring adventure, or nothing.   Helen Keller

---

Can you imagine what would happen in Australia if thousands of employees, each in his or her own way, started to take some small steps of responsibility to ensure the success of their organisations? Organisational success in any field, whether it is in business, sport, politics or charity, is determined by the number of team members who are willing to take responsibility and to be accountable. Yet so many people seem unwilling or unable to do so. How can this resistance be overcome? As we have already discussed, passion is the source of courage; it enables us to do difficult things, to take risks and to live 'the life of daring' that Helen Keller challenges us to live. When we are passionate about something, we care enough to take responsibility.

It doesn't matter whether you're the big cheese or a cubicle rat . . . It doesn't matter whether you command a legion of minions, or only your Palm Pilot. All that matters is whether you care enough to start from where you are! . . . So ask yourself: Do you care so much about the magnificent difference that you can make in this world that you're willing to try and change it with your bare heart?   Gary Hamel

---

So, stop waiting for the government to do something. Stop waiting for your chairman to do something. Stop waiting for 'big business' to do something. Stop waiting for 'them' to do something. It's really up to you and to me. And it's up to each person who can see one small step that should be taken. Do what you, with your unique insights and knowledge, think needs to be done. Do what you are passionate about. The responsibility that you are then willing to take on will indeed change our world, and become an inspiration to those around you.

Creativity and innovation

Creativity and innovation are critical success factors in the fast-changing global business environment of the twenty-first century.

My friend and professional speaking colleague, Ed Bernacki, wrote a fascinating book, *Wow! That's a great idea!* He says there are two types of companies:

- those that welcome new, creative ideas; learn from them; are not scared of the changes that new ideas may require; and are led by people who are not threatened by those who find new or better ways to do things
- those that don't welcome ideas or new ways of thinking about the organisation.

Gary Hamel, in his preface to *Leading the Revolution* said:

I found that the most successful companies weren't obsessed with their competitors; instead they were following the polestar of some truly noble aspiration. What counted was not so much how they positioned themselves against long-standing rivals, but how creatively they used their core competencies to create entirely new markets . . . Only those companies that are capable of creating industry revolutions will prosper in the new economy.

Leaders who are not passionate will not be able to create the necessary environment for creativity and innovation. Their organisations will struggle to simply stay with the pack, let alone stand out. Innovation and creativity both require the same mind-set. A willingness to take risks and make mistakes. And great leaders understand the need to reward mistakes! This sounds a bit scary, but we live in fast-changing times. Human beings are designed to learn through trial and error. Unless you and your employees are learning new skills, new attitudes and new ideas, you will be left behind.

Anyone who has never made a mistake has never tried anything new.
Albert Einstein

The tragedy is that employees are often punished for making mistakes. They were punished in school, and now they see colleagues lose their jobs for making mistakes. Empassioned employees, however, will be able to find the necessary courage to overcome this past pattern of learning—and leaders must encourage them to do so.

In my view, there are two types of mistakes—skill mistakes and attitude mistakes. *Skill mistakes* are those caused by the lack of necessary skills or knowledge. For example:
- research and development errors
- mistakes in 'closing' sales
- mistakes in designing a marketing or strategic plan.

Skill mistakes occur despite best intentions or an excellent attitude. Like a serious sportsperson, sometimes we need to make repeated skill mistakes before we ultimately master the skill. These mistakes should not be punished.

By contrast, *attitude mistakes* are those where the person's state of mind causes the mistake. These mistakes must not be repeated—they must be eliminated as quickly as possible. Examples are:

- not arriving at team meetings on time
- not caring enough to solve customers' problems
- abusing or harassing other team members.

So, stay at the forefront of business and technology by sharing and rewarding skill mistakes—they are learning experiences. As Herb Kelleher, CEO of Southwest Airlines, said in an interview:

If people are doing things that are adventuresome, if they're doing things that are outside the box, if they're doing things that are visionary, and they fail at doing them, we compliment them for the attitude and the perception and the sense of adventure and curiosity and inquiry that brought those things to pass. And that builds up confidence in them.

The dark side of passion

I have been discussing the virtues of passion for organisations and leaders. It is important to remember, however, that passion—whether for a person, a thing, an organisation or an ideal—can be destructive. Unless passion is tempered by reason, as Gibran advocates, it soon turns from a virtue into a deadly sin.

No matter how passionate we are, it is vital to maintain a sense of perspective. While passion can be a force that drives us through all obstacles, it can also blind us to reality and make us lose sight of the bigger picture. It can drive innovation, but it can also stifle creativity and be the death of serendipity. In an organisational setting, it can result in blinkered thinking, bloody-mindedness, short-term or opportunist thinking, misplaced energy, questionable behaviour and the destruction of teams.

The keys to avoiding the dark side of passion are perspective and self-awareness (of actions, feelings and consequences). In a work setting, the following are clues that passion is becoming an obsession:

- You become addicted to work.
- Following the passion is no longer enjoyable or energising; instead it is a compulsion.

- The object of passion is of greater importance than the relationships that are dear to you.
- You ignore your physical health.
- You ignore the wellbeing of those you lead.
- To further your aims, you make demands on others that cause them harm.
- You believe that only your own goals and aims matter.
- You are willing to sacrifice your ethics, values and integrity in order to achieve the object of your passion.
- Your passion becomes an end in itself, instead of a means to achieve your higher purpose.

Passionate alignment

The passionate performance 'sweet spot' occurs when a leader is able to generate passion at all levels of the organisation and *align it*. That is, the passion of all team members is aligned with that of the leader and the organisation. When this occurs, the true benefits of teamwork can appear—*synergy* happens.

'Synergy' is what occurs when the behaviour of the whole is unpredicted by the sum of the parts. Dr R Buckminster Fuller

---

Synergy is what coaches of world-class sporting teams achieve. That is, when the hearts, minds and bodies of team members contribute to the group's goals. In organisational terms, this is called alignment. So, how can you align the passion and purpose of each individual with the purpose of the organisation? The first step is to create clarity around the following terms:
- purpose or mission
- vision
- goals
- values
- strategy.

Most employees of organisations with whom I have conducted workshops have little concept of what their leader thinks these five terms mean. And yet they are amongst the most powerful resources a leader can use to engage the hearts and minds of team members. When they are clarified, in simple terms that can be remembered, employees can engage with them, and can see how their own purpose can be pursued whilst pursuing organisational purpose.

Often, a leader will define the terms and publish them, but nothing happens after that. Following the lead of sporting coaches is instructive in this instance. Understand the need for constant and never-ending repetition and discussion of the meaning and relevance of the terms.

You, as a leader at any level, can play a role in changing corporate culture to support passion in the workplace, by understanding the power of alignment, and applying it with your team. Don't wait for the CEO to do this work! Extract the relevant information from published corporate materials and use it. When your team starts to generate better results, your colleagues will begin to emulate your example.

On the issue of 'values', many organisations have invested in discovering, adopting and then publishing corporate values, but then proceed to ignore them on a day-to-day basis. If something is happening in your organisation that is contrary to the values it publicises (for example, in marketing or internal documents), then you, as the leader, are responsible for doing something about it. And you, as a leader, are also responsible for giving your followers opportunities to discuss, explore and complain about the proper application of corporate values to daily activities. Those whom you lead want to follow you. They want to be inspired by you, and motivated by you. Make a decision to become truly passionate about the highest purpose of your organisation, and your followers will *feel* your leadership at a soul level, rather than just as a mental exercise of more corporate theory. Regardless of how large a team you lead, the power of passion can be communicated down the line.

In summary, the keys to passionate alignment are clarity and simplicity around purpose, vision and goals, and understanding the need for repetition and the power of you personally sharing the message. The process I am suggesting to achieve this is:
• Clarify the game the organisation is playing.
• Clarify the rules of the game.

- Show the players the benefit to themselves of succeeding in the game.
- Reinforce the messages constantly.
- Discuss with the team problems that they identify.
- Give recognition for good work.
- Celebrate wins along the way.

Uncovering passion

I believe that finding, and then pursuing, your passion is the key to a life that will fulfil you, nourish you and, almost inevitably, give you a feeling of being 'successful'. Because your passion comes from your soul or spirit, and is not a mental process, peeling away the layers of your past learning and experience and the judgments of others is often difficult. But it's oh so rewarding! How do you do it? And how can you help others to uncover their passion?

Personal purpose

What is the 'purpose' of your life? Why were you born? What are the foundational issues upon which you base your every decision? What is important to you (these are often described as 'values')? I believe that answering these questions is a vital ingredient in living a life that will make us all feel successful. And passion is a clue to your life purpose.

- The things that you are passionate about are the 'street signs' to your life purpose.
- You are meant to be pursuing these things, and by pursuing them to discover the true purpose of your life.
- Your passion gives you the direction, and whilst pursuing that direction, you have a greater chance of discovering the real reasons why you are alive.

What you consider to be 'good' and 'bad' in your life depends on what you have discovered your life purpose to be. If *you* don't decide this for yourself, then you may be seduced into following the views of others, leading to the pursuit of perceived 'good' things that can't fulfil you. That, in my view, is a wasted life, a life of unfulfilled potential.

If you wish to help others to find their passion, first you must have done the work to find your own. And you must indeed be pursuing it. You can then inspire those you lead to take the risk of discovering passion.

Self-knowledge and the soul

Great leaders throughout history, such as Mahatma Gandhi, Nelson Mandela, Jesus, Buddha and Mohammed, have all taught that we grow in wisdom through increased self-knowledge.

There is no need to run outside for better seeing . . .
Rather abide at the centre of your being;
For the more you leave it, the less you learn.
Search your heart and see
The way to do is to be.   Lao Tzu

Self-knowledge will also help you to peel back the layers of experience and learning and discover your purpose and passion. By then pursuing your purpose and passion, you will increase your knowledge and understanding of your 'self'—truly the path to wisdom.

Your soul (spirit or heart, if you prefer) is the part of you that is neither mind nor body. It is the essential part of you that is unchanging. Accessing your soul or spirit is accessing the real you, and this is the key to gaining self-knowledge.

Research indicates that when people retire and look back on their lives they say one of two things. One: I regret not spending more time with my children. Two: I regret not doing something for my soul.   Paul Clitheroe

---

I believe that your passion is sourced from your soul (or spirit or heart). It energises you, and enables you to strive for, and ultimately achieve, excellence. If you allow it, your soul can guide you along the path of 'right conduct'. Your passion, in turn, gives you the strength to 'do the right thing', and to act in a moral way. How can you access your soul (and therefore your 'self' and passion)? Consider these steps:
1. Pursue those things about which you are passionate!
2. Spend time with your loved ones.

3. Spend time outdoors with nature, even if it is only in the garden.
4. Learn to meditate, and then do it regularly.
5. Make a community contribution.
6. Read books on spirituality to learn spiritual exercises that are not necessarily religious.
7. If you are religious, pray. If not, spend time reviewing and giving thanks for the things in your life for which you have reason to be grateful.

Steps for uncovering passion

Every person is passionate about at least one thing. Yet so many people tell me they can't identify what it is they are passionate about. In my first book, *Passionate People Produce*, I developed a process to help people find or recover their passion. This is a summary of the first two steps of this process.

Step 1: The seeker

The *seeker* makes a decision to seek his or her passion. You cannot find your passion by hoping it will just turn up somewhere. It takes an act of will—and then discipline—to decide to find and pursue your passion. Somewhat like running a marathon, it is necessary to *decide* to commence the process. The blockage to finding passion can be significant, primarily because our experience and learning have covered our true selves, and unless we *want* to find our passion, we are easily thwarted.

I have found that only when I truly *want* something do I exercise my will to take the necessary actions.

Step 2: The detective

The *detective* then takes steps to look into the past:
- He explores the times that he had spontaneous enthusiasms and interests.
- She interviews people who knew her when she was passionate.
- They find clues that help to resolve the puzzle of where their passion lies.

So how would you do this? Start by asking yourself some hard questions.

- What makes me angry?
- What do I love?
- What did I love doing as a child?
- What would I be doing if I had $10 million in the bank and didn't need to worry about money?
- For what activities do I have unlimited energy?
- For what would I sacrifice my life?

As you look inside you will start to understand what makes you 'tick' (and you will also be able to apply this understanding to others).

When passion is missing

If you as a leader are not passionate, then you must either take a risk in your life and leave your existing role, or take steps to rekindle your passion. The latter course is possible, even if the passion died a long time ago.

Rekindling passion

Here are some strategies to rekindle your passion, or to maintain it. These strategies apply both to you as a leader and to your followers.

- Remember how you felt when you first joined your organisation, and why you chose to work there.
- Understand that conflict with others, including your own leaders, is a natural part of life. Perhaps you have focused too much on the pain attached to the conflicts, rather than the pleasures of your role.
- Be grateful for the 'good' parts of your role, and the benefits your income creates in your life outside of work. We can tend to focus too much on the negatives, and thereby forget the positives!
- Read the corporate purpose, vision, goals and values statements every day, to remind yourself of the spiritual elements of your work, of the impact that your work is having on other human beings.
- Lighten up! Unless you are involved in medical or emergency services, it is probable that your work is not a matter of life and

death. If you lose your job, you will not die. Worrying unnecessarily will surely kill your passion for your role and will limit your contribution. Increase the levels of fun you create at work—follow the advice in the chapter in this book on humour. I believe that fun is a spiritual experience, and the more fun your team has, the more profitable it can be.

- Understand that every person's unique picture of reality and their unique personality mean that the behaviour of others will require constant interpretation. Learn to understand others' values, concepts and issues. Learn to accept that a differing opinion is not a personal rejection. This is the key to alignment with the corporate purpose and is, once again, what great teams do. They appreciate their different views, and generate synergy from the exploration of seeming conflict.

Coping in a dispassionate environment

What if you are passionate about what you are doing, but are in a passion-adverse environment or culture? My first suggestion is that you understand your personal responsibility for changing the environment. Your personal power is not a function of formal authority. If you truly understand the power of passion, you would not stand by and accept the squashing of passion!

My second suggestion is to continue to access and demonstrate your passion, despite the challenges and criticisms for doing so. Undoubtedly you will have a ripple-like impact on others as they observe your behaviours, particularly if you are their leader. In fact, this is what it means to act like a leader, regardless of official titles. Inspire those around you with your passion.

On the other hand, if you are worn out from the challenge, your ultimate and most powerful step is to leave a dispassionate leader and environment. The price you pay for remaining is far too great in my opinion; it detrimentally affects your mental, physical and spiritual wellbeing. I challenge you with this question: Is money more important to you than your emotional and physical health?

Conclusion

Who are the great leaders? What makes a great leader? Do any of the current political leaders inspire you with their energy? Do any of them demonstrate the leadership qualities that you believe are important? Do our leaders impress you with their ability to tell the truth?

I believe we have too many 'wimps' who hold leadership positions in Australia—in business, in politics (on all sides) and in sport. They are wimps because they don't have the courage to say what they really believe!

Where is Australia heading? What's the vision for this wonderful country? For some time now, none of the leaders of Australia's major parties have articulated a passionately-held vision that could inspire a nation to look further than next week's pay cheque! After the Sydney Olympics in 2000, which inspired, motivated and galvanised us to achieve so much and with such success, to what do we as a nation aspire?

My vision is an Australia in the year 2020 with a population that is double its size in 2000, where our well-recognised sense of fair play and tolerance will ensure a successful nation regardless of the origin of our people. The only way we can achieve this challenging and scary target is with a passionate commitment to growth and migration, to an understanding that it is human energy and human spirit that is the key to a nation's prosperity. Such an attitude derives from a positive, giving, growing perspective rather than from the negative, fear-filled perspective of building fortress Australia.

Are the actions I recommend simple? Yes. Are they easy? No.

I am convinced that passion is a virtue. It changes lives for the better. Are you willing to take the necessary responsibility? The choice is yours.

What is a passionate leader?

1 Passionate leaders *are clear about their purpose.*
2 Passionate leaders *have unlimited amounts of energy.*
3 Passionate leaders *have courage.*
4 Passionate leaders *inspire others.*
5 Passionate leaders *are creative and innovative.*
6 Passionate leaders *build great teams.*
7 Passionate leaders *have learned the need for self-awareness that leads to wisdom.*

Strategies for personal passionate performance

1 Write out your *goals* in the areas of mind, body and spirit.
2 Accept that you create your own *unique* picture of reality.
3 Know yourself! *Self-knowledge* is the key to wisdom.
4 Access your *courage* to take risks and make mistakes.
5 Be willing to be *uniquely* you.
6 Invest 5 per cent of your time and income in your own *learning*, growth and development.
7 Take *responsibility* for your life. Don't blame other people.

Seven strategies for passionate leadership

1 Create an *inspirational* corporate purpose and vision.
2 Decide the *values* of the organisation, and then live by them.
3 *Balance* mind, body and spirit in the workplace.
4 Adopt clear rules to handle *mistakes.*
5 Accept and encourage the *uniqueness* of each person.
6 Invest in *learning*, growth and development.
7 Show *loyalty* to employees.

For further exploration

I have considered which books would be most likely to 'provoke' you along the passionate path. It's a difficult choice out of the many available, but I recommend the following:

—Anthony De Mello, *Awareness,* Image Books, New York, 1992.
   This is the best book I have read on the concepts of self-awareness, consciousness and reality. It's also short and easy to read!

—Dr R Buckminster Fuller, *Critical Path,* St Martin's Press, New York, 1981.
   Buckminster Fuller died in 1983 after being awarded 47 honorary degrees by universities around the world. My world view changed dramatically after reading this book. 'Bucky' (as he was affectionately known) said the future of Earth depends upon each and every person acting according to his or her intuition.

—Dr Joseph Murphy, *The Power of Your SubConscious Mind: One of the Most Powerful Self-Help Guides Ever Written!*, Pocket Books, London, 2000.
   I learned more about my mind, both conscious and subconscious, and its juxtaposition with the soul, from this book than from any other. Once again, I love it because it's refreshingly short.

WISDOM 7

Dexter Dunphy and Tyrone Pitsis

About the authors

Dexter Dunphy, BA (Hons), DipEd, MEd (Hons), PhD (Sociology)

After graduating from Sydney University Dexter taught in state schools then went on to complete a PhD at Harvard University. He stayed in the USA for six years, teaching, researching and writing about group dynamics and organisations. He also became increasingly involved in leading personal growth groups.

Dexter returned to a Senior Lectureship in Sociology at the University of NSW. In 1972 he gave the ABC's prestigious Boyer lectures on 'The Challenge of Change'. He moved on to the Australian Graduate School of Management as a Professor of Management, and more recently to the University of Technology, Sydney, as Distinguished Professor.

He has published 18 books and 70 articles, consulted to over 150 organisations in Australia and overseas, taught at universities around the globe, and received awards for scholarship. (He is about to publish the first collection of his poems—a brave act!) He has also helped to train many corporate and community leaders.

Dexter's first commitment has been to his spiritual development and that of others; to creating human workplaces and to caring for this planet. He has had, and continues to have, a profoundly fulfilling life.

Dextex Dunphy can be reached at dexter.dunphy@uts.edu.au.

Tyrone S Pitsis, BSocSc (Policy), BSc (Hons) (Psychology)

Tyrone grew up as a child of Greek migrants in Sydney's Newtown. He dropped out of school at 14 and eventually found a job as a kitchen hand. He went on to become an executive chef who, after one too many 80-hour weeks and no formal education, decided to study for the Higher School Certificate at TAFE New South Wales.

While working as a chef he completed an honours degree with distinction from the University of New South Wales, then began his academic career at the Australian Graduate School of Management. Recently he joined the Innovative Collaborations, Alliances and Networks (ICAN) Research Centre at the University of Technology, Sydney.

Tyrone lectures in organisational behaviour in the MBA program at UTS and conducts research into organisational culture and leadership development. He has published papers in top management journals and at conferences he has been recipient of best paper awards. He is a member of the American Academy of Management and the first Australian to be elected chair of the Academy's new Doctoral Student Consortium (2002–3). He is currently working on a PhD thesis investigating the role of emotion in leadership decision-making, and specialising in relationship breakdown.

A kitchen hand to an award-winning researcher—anything is possible!

Tyrone Pitsis can be reached at tyrone.pitsis@uts.edu.au.

Introduction

Surprisingly, wisdom is not widely mentioned in management and leadership circles today. As far as we know, there isn't a single course in any management school with the title 'Wisdom'—not even a 'Wisdom 101'. But cursory reading of the business press on a day-to-day basis seems to point to the need for more wisdom on the part of our corporate leaders.

This chapter seeks to map a path that the seeker of wisdom can travel. We begin this journey by asking what appears to be a simple question.

What is wisdom?

According to the *Concise Oxford Dictionary*:

Wisdom is the possession of experience and knowledge together with the power of applying them critically or practically.

The central idea in this definition is that wisdom, knowledge and experience are fused in decisions and expressed through action. Decisions are 'wise' when they take into account the wider context and are not made on some more limited base for judgment such as egoism, prejudice or intellectual understanding alone.

Wisdom is also expressed in 'wise sayings'. We can access the wisdom of others through proverbs, stories and aphorisms handed down through one or more wisdom traditions. These represent the accumulated wisdom of centuries of human experience. Yet there is no short cut to wisdom—we must test the truth of these sayings for ourselves in the hot human process of life for them to be meaningful for us.

Knowledge alone is not wisdom. Neither is experience. The two must be fused experientially so that they are transformed and complement each other. But even together, knowledge and experience amount to little unless they flow into action—action that makes a difference in the world in some positive way.

Wisdom is the fruit of a life lived fully and mindfully; the result of learning from experience and changing ourselves rather than simply repeating the habitual responses programmed into us in our early lives. We are not born wise; we must acquire wisdom. Yet few of us become truly wise. Why?

At the personal level, we are taught to conform to the prevailing norms—to fit in; not to question too much; not to 'rock the boat'. When we live unreflectively on 'hand-me-down' values, we are simply automatons, programmed by the prejudices of others. By contrast, maturity and wisdom come from first accepting responsibility for deciding who we wish to be, and then reprogramming ourselves accordingly.

A major barrier to becoming wise is *fear*—fear of not being accepted or acceptable. Fear prevents us from drawing direct conclusions from our own experience and from critically evaluating the judgments of others. To become wise, therefore, we must dare to be different. Not just for the sake of being different, but so that we are free to respond creatively from the fullness of our whole being.

Wisdom is not about being perfect—it is about being whole and choosing the life that is the deepest expression of our humanity. Wisdom comes from being pushed out of our comfort zone and having our customary ways of perceiving the world challenged or shattered. It's about learning to cope with anything and rising like the phoenix out of the ashes. Reflection on such experiences is also a source of wisdom. Much of modern life, however, is a distraction from that prerequisite for wisdom, reflection—contemplation of apparent disasters, the mystery of life and death, and our own relative insignificance in the universe.

Instant wisdom

We live in what Stan Davis has called the age of the 'blur'. In the information age everything moves faster than the ability of our human information processing system to cope. We no longer have time to sit and think about what we heard, saw, smelled or felt. We are bombarded with a torrent of information, much of which is merely meaningless data unless placed within a larger interpretive scheme.

If we search for a scheme to make sense of all of this data, however, we are faced with a plethora of competing alternatives. For example, every profession has developed its own systematic way of turning data into information and knowledge. Political viewpoints and commercial interests also vie in offering us ready made, prepackaged alternative interpretations of reality. In particular, science has become the religion of the age—but unfortunately a version of science that regards 'spirituality' with suspicion and relegates 'values' to the occasional unpopular ethics course. Zohar and Marshall sum it up well in their comment: 'We live in a spiritually dumb culture'.

The speed of change also challenges the relevance of traditional sources of wisdom—family, community, religion, the arts and philosophy. They and the past are seen as an inadequate guide for what will be a dramatically different future. In the contemporary world there is an emphasis on novelty, which leads to fads and 'instant wisdom'. Fads are a superficial response to the genuine novelty of the emerging world, but eventually they disappoint us because they lack the power to create effective action—action that nourishes us and the world, and action that is sustainable and sustaining.

Unfortunately there is no magic pill to make us wise—no quick fix. The path to wisdom is a journey, but often a difficult one, so many turn back. This journey, however, is critical to our spiritual life.

Wisdom and leadership

The purpose of life is to give birth to oneself.   Erich Fromm

The journey to wisdom can follow many paths, some of which pass through the challenging realm of work and, in particular, managing. After all, the work of managers requires merging knowledge and experience and then applying them through action. However, our choice of a wisdom-path is basically arbitrary and ultimately of no great significance. It matters little whether we choose to seek wisdom by travelling the path of a manager, a potter, a tennis player or a clown. What matters is that we pursue wisdom with integrity and tenacity and that we are prepared to engage in the exacting discipline that is the only basis of true wisdom. But because managerial leadership is so central to modern society, so difficult and demanding an activity, and presents us with so many challenges, it is a worthy path to mastery and wisdom.

In the past, many practical pursuits were organised collectively so that beginners could gain the relevant knowledge and 'skills of the trade' and be progressively introduced to the discipline of the activity. For example, stonemasons, goldsmiths and weavers were organised into guilds. Within the guilds, initiation rites and transition through increasing levels of skill were designed to create the spiritual discipline needed to develop the wisdom associated with true mastery. Ideally, the master craftspeople were highly developed spiritual beings as well as skilled workers. Part of their role was to develop other younger artisans as they moved along their path to mastery.

Today, we lack this systematic approach. As managerial leaders, we usually have to create our own path to wisdom, helped along by the occasional model or mentor on a spare-time basis.

The progress to mastery

But if the path to wisdom leads to mastery, then how do we gain mastery? Table 7.1 outlines the stages necessary to gain mastery of the skills of managerial leadership.

The novice—learning 'the rules'

Many people become novice leaders almost imperceptibly, and usually without apparent choice. The engineer who finds that three to four years out of university she must manage a sizeable project—something her engineering degree did not prepare her for. Or the accountant who finds himself promoted to head the accounting section.

Many people embark on a management path unwittingly and somewhat reluctantly, feeling out of their depth. As they progress down the path they find that the basis of their security, their traditional non-managerial basis of expertise, is more and more out of date and irrelevant to what they are doing. Therefore, when they finally *choose* the leadership path, they search for a set of rules to guide their action. At this stage established rules are important. Knowledge and action require routinised, standardised and formalised procedures. At first the novice clings to the rules for security, but over time learns that established rules do not always work.

The advanced beginner—beyond rules to strategy

The novice then becomes the *advanced beginner*. As she acquires more experience, she discovers that managerial leadership is complex and the rules she formerly relied on are over-simplifications.

Table 7.1: Stages in achieving leadership mastery

Stage	Nature
1. Novice—learning 'the rules'	• We seek clear guidelines on how to act in different situations. • We observe the codified knowledge of others who have been managerial leaders.
2. Advanced beginner—beyond rules to strategy	• We realise that in many situations, the rules don't work. • Making change is more complex than we thought. • Rules are evolved into thoughtful strategies.
3. Competence—disciplined effectiveness	• We develop a 'feel' for the complexity of the meaningful world. • We select cues and respond to them on the basis of our accumulating experience. • Our knowledge now is more tacit; our strategies are evolving to include deeper levels of awareness.
4. Proficiency—fluid, effortless performance	• We have internalised the strategies and they are backed up with high levels of skill. • Intuition now dominates and reason is secondary.
5. Mastery—acting from our deepest intuition with confidence and flow	• We become one with the changes we are making and that are changing our organisational world and ourselves simultaneously. • Our inner and outer worlds are one. • What we do often seems effortless and spontaneous.

Rules now evolve into *strategies* and thought processes. 'Yes, but the rules for appraisal I have learned must be modified when I am dealing with stubborn defensiveness in the person being appraised. In these circumstances, my strategy is . . .'. The outcome is the cumulative building of expertise—knowledge grounded in experience.

Competence—disciplined effectiveness

We realise the world is not rational; it is complex, ambiguous and highly uncertain. Therefore, we seek certainty through our experience and expertise and we select and respond to cues on the basis of these experiences. We begin to make sense of the relationship between our decisions, our actions and our environment. However, the solutions we find depend on the depth of our expertise—our *competence*.

Figure 7.1 shows the kinds of competencies that leaders use on a day-to-day basis when they reach this stage and which are critical to progression to the higher stages of proficiency and mastery.

Figure 7.1: Skills of effective leaders

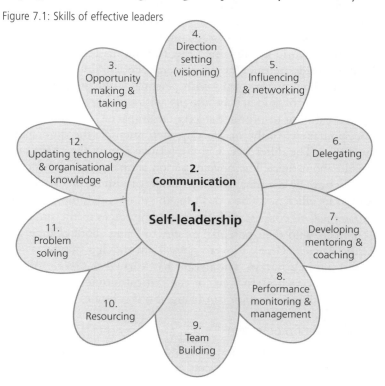

Each of the 'petals' in the flower diagram represents a key interpersonal or task competency. They overlap and interrelate with each other. But all of them are embedded in, and depend on, the two core competencies of *self-leadership* and *communication*.

Proficiency—fluid, effortless performance

The next stage is *proficiency*—a high level of competence based on a fusion of knowledge with experience. The evidence for the attainment of proficiency is *effortless performance*.

Rules and strategies are now deeply internalised so that a disciplined intuition dominates and reason is secondary. The proficient professional can explain his behaviour—but only on reflection after the fact.

Mastery

The final step is to become a master; that is, to act from your deepest intuition with confidence and flow.

The master goes beyond ego and personal identity to become one with the organising process, changing herself and the organisational world at the same time. For the master, the inner and outer worlds are one; they are interdependent and overlapping. The master speaks with personal authority and economy of words, and acts minimally with effortless spontaneity and perfect timing to produce maximum impact.

The spontaneity of the master can often resemble the spontaneity of the novice. The difference is in the relative impact they have on the world about them. The novice's action is hit and miss. The master's action, by contrast, is calm, reliable, persistent, precise and elegant in its efficiency. The reason for the differential impact is that the master acts in concert with the unfolding forces in the situation and connects with their potential energy to bring about change.

As the Ancient Greek proverb goes: 'I am moving slowly because I am in a hurry'. The master has learned the secret of 'not doing' and knows how to wait for the critical moment when what may be a small intervention can bring about substantial change.

The challenge of progression

Progression through the roles discussed, and the consequent gaining of wisdom, is by no means automatic. Each stage is fraught with difficulty and requires us to overcome increasing challenges. These challenges usually appear to be external, but they are always, ultimately, internal. They depend on us making spiritual progress—what Carlos Casteneda calls *abandoning the fortress of the self.* There is usually a crisis at the transition point between the stages, because the transition to the next stage involves the apparent sacrifice of much that has been learned before. In reality, you get to keep that which you let go, but this is only apparent later.

- In moving from the *novice* and *advanced beginner* stages, we have to 'give up' our reliance on the very rules that we have spent so much time acquiring and which have provided a sense of security in a confusing world.
- To progress from the *expert* stage, we must abandon the highly organised world of the specialty that has provided standing, status and certainty.
- If we are to move on from the *professional* stage, we must learn that the proficiency in which we formerly took such pride was an illusion. To become a *mast*er, we must plunge into the mystery of the unknown again.
- As *master* we have learnt to live with resistance to ideas that are often seen as radical. We accept that things are as they are, and only by understanding this can change occur. For a time we will, invariably, be an outcast from the communities from which we came. We know that the sacrifices we make in the short term are far outweighed by the positive outcomes in the future—outcomes that will continue long after we are gone.

A cautionary note

There are many who would rather seek wisdom from others than try to find it within themselves—who hope to avoid the traps we have just described by complete reliance on a guru or master. The fact that masters or gurus are often useful sources of wisdom leaves the seeker open to potential manipulation.

In *Feet of Clay—A Study of Gurus,* Anthony Storr discusses a number of well-known gurus, some of whom were lethal and others who were largely benign. His case studies include Jim

Jones, David Koresh, Rajneesh, Steiner, Jung, Freud, Ignatius of Loyola, Paul Brunton and Mother Meera. Jim Jones, for example, set up Jim Jones People's Temple in Jonestown, Guyana. On 18 November 1978, on Jones's orders, over 900 people (including 260 children) in this community voluntarily drank, or were forcibly injected with, cyanide.

Notwithstanding, all the people Storr deals with aspired to be 'masters' in the sense we have described it in this chapter. They claimed special insight—a unique source for their wisdom—and they were fluent and effective communicators. The danger, as Storr illustrates, is that gurus attract followers, particularly amongst those who seek certainty but lack confidence in their own ability to find it in themselves.

Self-surrender to a guru can relieve the follower from the burden of personal responsibility. Rather than seeking their own wisdom, followers submit to the authority of the guru, adopting his or her wisdom as their own. This is particularly dangerous when the guru is introverted, narcissistic, power-oriented and psychologically disturbed.

Ten guidelines for those seeking wisdom

As we have indicated, the road to mastery is extremely difficult and fraught with danger. There are, however, some guidelines to the 'getting of wisdom' that you can use. These appear simple, but are actually extremely difficult to adhere to. They take practice, commitment and persistence. They require you to:

1. Know yourself and the source of your power.
2. Live in the now.
3. Concentrate on 'seeing'.
4. Accept reality in order to change it.
5. Choose your domain of action.
6. Know what you want to bring about in that domain.
7. Engage the world actively, but with discernment.
8. Understand that people and relationships are primary.
9. Listen to others and communicate with purpose, precision and power.
10. Celebrate life in its success and adversity.

Know yourself

As far as we can discern, the sole purpose of human existence is to kindle a light in the darkness of mere being.   Carl Jung

The journey to self-discovery is about finding who we really are and who we may become. We sense that this is no idle commitment and that the journey will not be an easy one—there are huge obstacles to be surmounted; the path is shrouded in forests and mists; there are undoubtedly adversaries to be encountered who will threaten our very existence. We hesitate. Is it worth it? Gradually we begin to understand that without threats and obstacles we cannot grow. They are necessary if we are to learn and so we need to treat them as challenges and opportunities for growth, not as problems to be avoided.

Ultimately we are the source of our own power, our own freedom and our own happiness. Self-knowledge allows us to take responsibility for our lives, to work with the material we have been given and to shape the self we aspire to be.

Live in the now

Carpe diem (seize the day)   Latin proverb

One of the characteristics of being a master is the ability to be fully aware of the present moment and its potential. A major obstacle for those of us seeking to travel the path to wisdom is that we live in the present with a mind map drawn in the past. Our inherited mind maps carry with them inbuilt action programs that have passed their 'use by' dates. They were once fresh and vibrant but have now exhausted their explanatory power.

To compound the issue further, we also live in the present with a mind map projected into the future that often ignores the present reality. A truly wise person understands his current situation, his strengths and limitations, and plans to change the future accordingly. He does not allow the baggage of the past to cloud his journey, nor does he allow the daydreams of his future to make him forget the present. The truly wise person lives in the now.

Vision without planning is a daydream; planning without vision is a nightmare.   Japanese proverb

Concentrate on 'seeing'

Mostly people do not perceive what is around them. People look at a flower and say: 'That is a rose', and believe that they have seen it. But the word offers only an illusion of knowledge. Every rose is unique; a marvellous world of varying colours, forms, textures and scents, and of memories, emotions, times and places. Labelling is not perceiving—in fact, labelling and stereotyping are antithetical to perceiving.

The progression to wisdom requires a commitment to detailed and full observation of ourselves and of the world about us; seeking to fully experience things without the distractions of expectations or stereotypes. When we observe another person, for example, we can tune in to many levels of information—the content of their words, their posture, all their non-verbal gestures and the intonations of their voice, their style of clothing. We all signal our dominant concerns through multiple channels and with considerable redundancy. We can observe ourselves in the same way.

Deikman writes of the 'observing self' from which comes our core sense of personal existence. Our understanding of who we are is located in our awareness itself and not in the content of what we observe. It is this observing self, Deikman argues, that allows us 'to awaken fully from the trance of ordinary life'.

The discipline of seeing or observing takes us progressively deeper into self-knowledge and allows us to penetrate the superficial surface of the socially constructed and accepted external 'reality'.

Accept reality in order to change it

Whenever I have come up against a blank wall, it turned out to be the gateway to a new opportunity.   Beverley Dunphy

Wisdom comes from acceptance that what is, is! It is very easy to confuse our fears with reality or, on the other hand, to imagine that what we hope for already exists. We can frighten ourselves with fantasies of disaster or delude ourselves with illusory dreams. Facing reality requires the rawest kind of courage—there is no other basis for effective action than the clear, cold light of reality.

Acceptance also means that we abandon the indulgence of self-pity; we stop wringing our hands about the state of the world; we relinquish the luxury of pretence. All these things mire us down and hold us back from resolute action; we develop what psychologists call learned helplessness.

By contrast, the path to wisdom is often described as the way of the warrior, or of the hunter or the sorcerer. It demands emotional discipline.

Choose your domain of action

None of us can play out the drama of our lives across all spheres of life. Wisdom comes from accepting this and choosing where we will make an impact. For the leader, this may be a choice of organisation, career path or country—or all three.

It is easy to imagine that working in what seems like a small niche relegates what we do to insignificance. And yet this is clearly not true. As far as we know, Jesus never left Palestine and yet his ideas changed the world. Nelson Mandela's prison cell probably didn't seem like much of a place to seek wisdom, let alone move the world.

When we refer to choice here, we do not mean that this is simply a cognitive process. Rather it is the kind of choice that goes beyond our rational cognitive mind to involve our emotional and spiritual intelligence.

One of the characteristics of leaders is that they:

. . . comprehend the emergence of great principles in apparently small things. They see larger processes behind small events. They have experienced transcendence in their own lives. Debashis Chatterjee

---

It is the quality of our action, not its sphere, which determines the impact we make. We do not have to occupy a lofty position to be a wise leader.

Know what you want to bring about in that domain

While it is important to accept the current reality as our starting point, leadership is the creation of new realities. This means that we must envision the future we want to bring into being.

In business, as in art, what distinguishes leaders from laggards and greatness from mediocrity, is the ability to uniquely imagine what could be.   Hamel and Prahalad

---

However, a warning is in order. Contrary to the nostrums in popular books on how to achieve success, wisdom is never simply satisfying our selfish ego—it encompasses *the greater good*. The achievement of selflessness opens us up to cooperate with the emergent forces generating the future. In this sense, we are only midwives of the future that is being born, not the shapers of it. We do not have to be able to envision it in detail; we only need to be responsive enough to allow it to work through us. And the change begins within us, as Mahatma Gandhi once said:

I must first be the change I want to bring about in the world.

In the earlier stages of the path to wisdom, as a novice or advanced beginner, much of what we do will be experimental for we are only learning about the world and ourselves. We need not be afraid of this. If life is a learning laboratory, everything we do and that happens to us becomes our teacher. There are no mistakes—only different ways of doing things that build our knowledge and skill and advance us further down the path of developing understanding and competence.

In retrospect, the blood, sweat and tears we experience often stem from our own resistance to changing ourselves—we are wrestling with our own shadow. When we become exhausted, stop resisting and let go, then we find we are caught up in the creative process. We learn to dance with the natural rhythms of the universe.

Engage the world actively, but with discernment

As leaders, we must know how to diagnose organisational problems and opportunities and how to intervene efficiently and skillfully. Leaders are often attracted to the role because they are doers who prefer action to analysis. The danger is that doers often mis-diagnose in their haste to act. There is no substitute for defining the problem or opportunity accurately for, without that, the intervention may make the problem worse or lead us to miss the opportunity.

Diagnosis is not simply a rational process. Insight into a confusing situation can come with a sudden 'aha' experience as the way we were viewing it suddenly shifts. Nothing may have changed in terms of the data we have at our disposal, or in the knowledge we bring to understanding the situation. But we have shifted our perspective.

It is easier for managerial leaders to acquire the skills of diagnosis and analysis than of intervention. Traditional MBA programs concentrate on diagnosis, particularly those that teach by the case method. However, few such programs teach intervention skills effectively and, in fact, skills of this kind cannot be taught in traditional classrooms. Intervention skills are mostly learned through apprenticeship and mentoring; on the job or by doing. In the end, doing is the ultimate test of wisdom for wisdom demands a full synthesis of all that we have learned as we progressed along the path to mastery.

There is a Greek saying: 'To catch fish, you must get your backside wet'. Despite the fact that our knowledge is almost always inadequate to the task, we must get involved in the action. The world of management is chaotic and messy. It is the leader's task to bring some productive order from the chaos—you don't find the fish and get them in the boat without getting wet. And it is action that tests the relevance and value of our knowledge. The world is engaged both through contemplation and through action.

To look is one thing
To see what you look at is another
To understand what you see is even more difficult
To learn from what you understand is something else again
But to act on what you learn is all that really matters.   Anon

---

Through action we forge the basis of our personal power (and in this context, power is not a four-letter word). The effective manager learns to act powerfully but responsibly—to use power for a larger purpose, not for self-aggrandisement. As managerial leaders, we need to understand where we can make a difference and where we can't. We can learn not to waste our energy where we can't make an impact and to focus it on where we can. And when we think we can make a difference, we need to act with power, efficiency and timing. The ability to do this comes with experience.

So the leader must lead—must be out in front when it is appropriate, model the emerging future in their own actions, clarify the vision and outline the path to it, inspire and enthuse others. But the great leader is also prepared to relinquish leadership to others; to identify others' strengths and help them awaken their own power and leadership capacity.

Great leaders do not make more followers; they make other leaders.

Greek proverb

Understand that people and relationships are primary

Organisations are deluged with technological innovations that sometimes offer dramatic new opportunities for increasing individual and corporate performance. Yet the more technologically dependent we are, the more important people become. Organisations and technology depend on people, and the more sophisticated the technology, the more knowledgeable and skilful the workforce needs to be to understand it and actualise its potential. Fundamentally, human relationships drive organisations and the quality of the relationships determines everything from the way the customer is treated to the quality of the products.

Organisations are not merely inert structures of units and departments but living fields of collective intelligence of the people who constitute the organisation.
Debashis Chatterjee

Therefore, leadership is about building value through effective relationships. Modern organisations no longer generate value primarily from physical assets, even in heavy industry. In the knowledge economy, they generate assets from ideas and competencies. The organisation can only do this effectively in a culture of trusting relationships, where people feel free to share ideas and transfer skills. There is no effective alternative, therefore, to treating employees as assets rather than costs; to helping them build their knowledge and competencies, and giving them a genuine stake in the business. To quote Chatterjee again: 'A corporation without the liberating spirit of community becomes a vicious circle of cold-hearted fortune seekers.'

Downsizing and exploitation are a scourge on society. Yet the leader is constantly faced with the need to use people as instruments in the pursuit of organisational goals; in one sense, he must do so because leadership is achieving things through people. Yet when we treat people only in this instrumental way, as means not ends, simply as assets to be deployed, allocated, downsized or terminated, then we miss the point of what organisations and leaders are for. Organisations and leaders are instruments of social purpose—they exist for people, not vice versa.

To live fully, we must learn to use things and love people, not love things and use people.
John Powell

Listen to others and communicate with purpose

Communication is a leader's central skill—all the other skills like influencing and team-building depend on it. The most neglected yet important aspect of communication is *listening* and a truly wise person lives by the dictum: 'How can I listen to you if I am thinking about what to say in response?'

Effective leaders spend a lot of time listening to others. And they build networks through which information flows to them about the concerns of the organisation's stakeholders. If they are in retailing, they walk the floors of their stores listening to what customers are saying. They stop and ask them questions, or put themselves into the customer's shoes. They formalise their inquiries with customer surveys. Similarly, they listen to their employees and ensure that information about how their employees are responding to changes is flowing through to them from all levels of the organisation. Again, the same is true for the unions, community groups, potential employees, suppliers and government officials.

Because they are persistent and effective listeners, wise leaders are seldom surprised by the views of those on whom the future welfare of the corporation depends. Wise leaders also keep others informed. They communicate clearly where the organisation is headed and what this means for all those in the organisation.

Communication is, however, more than words. A master's primary means of communication is by example—modelling in his or her behaviour the values and attitudes needed for the organisation to survive and thrive. The words and behaviour of the master are mutually supportive in their integrity and consistency. Walking the talk is more powerful than engaging in talk alone.

The communication of wisdom is concerned with something other than the transmission of information or even knowledge. Wisdom is directed to bringing about connection, enlightenment, inspiration and transformation. Wisdom is where the chasm between art, science and spirituality is filled. It must therefore speak to the minds, hearts and spirits of others.

Celebrate life in its success and adversity

The emotional side of wisdom is joy or bliss. The master has stepped out of the anxiety and fear that come from identifying with the ego. Her self has been enlarged to encompass humanity as a whole and is deeply connected to the soul of the earth itself, the source of life. The world, which once seemed threatening and threadbare, now seems supportive and a vast cornucopia of resources and possibilities. In this psychological space, it is natural to experience delight and a deep joy.

> *To see the world in a grain of sand*
> *And heaven in a wild flower,*
> *Hold infinity in the palm of your hand*
> *And eternity in an hour.*
>
> William Blake

Success grows out of wisdom and reinforces it. Wisdom and success become self-reinforcing attractors that amplify the emerging and evolving patterns of activity. But success is often hard won and cannot be defined only in terms of popularly acceptable outcomes.

The ultimate success is the progressive development of our own intellectual, emotional and spiritual development and contributing to others' development in the process. And sometimes that is the only success we have for a time—our goals for achievement in the external world often seem far off; we lose battles along the way; we experience our actions as fruitless. In such a situation it is easy to sink into despair and cynicism. The master knows, however, that it is the inner journey that matters and those who say 'yes' to life contribute to the future whatever the immediate outcomes. It is precisely at these times that it is important to celebrate, and to celebrate with others.

From the celebration of success and adversity, genuine community can emerge—a community of common purpose that generates new meaning. As the community grows in strength, it is natural to celebrate. The celebration is simply a welling-up of the shared joy in progressing the task at hand—a task which both accomplishes something of worth in itself and contributes to the creation of a culture supportive of human development.

Understand where this can lead

Of organisations there are three kinds. First, there are those that are organised on the basis of the power, wealth or authority of great leaders. Second, there are those that are organised because of convenience to the members, which will continue to exist as long as the members satisfy their convenience and do not quarrel. Third, there are those that are organised with some good teaching at its centre and harmony as its very life.

Of course, the third or last of these is the only true organisation, for in it the members live in one spirit from which the unity of spirit and various kinds of virtue will arise. In such an organisation will prevail harmony, satisfaction and happiness. The Teachings of Buddha

---

We are moving into an age where we need a transition from a corporate culture of greed to one of values-based action. The task of the corporation is to be a creator of value, not just of economic wealth, and a trustee acting responsibly to preserve value for the benefit of future generations. This shift is beginning to happen; it is as yet tentative and piecemeal and is still vigorously opposed by those whose interests are entrenched in maintaining the status quo. But it is happening, and we all have the choice of being part of the transformation; the agents of change. The challenge for all leaders is to be harbingers of the new order rather than relics of a fading past. This is a task that requires great courage, but as every change agent knows:

Like the turtle, to make progress we must stick our neck out.

Thai proverb

The seven deadly sins of leadership

Wisdom transcends religion, gender, age, generation, sexual orientation, culture and any other form of identifier that seeks to categorise people and societies. Similarly, the notion of deadly sins is inherent in all major religions and philosophies.

We have chosen the seven deadly sins from the Western tradition because they capture the essence of the critical *barriers* we experience as we pursue wisdom. The sins are:

1. Gluttony
2. Greed
3. Envy
4. Lust
5. Vanity
6. Wrath
7. Sloth

Each of the seven sins, singly or in combination, can entrap us so that we are distracted from our endeavour—the pursuit of wisdom. To help us recognise and avoid them, we will define each one and provide concrete examples of how they may entrap us.

But first a warning. Reading about what the 'ideal' leader does may make you feel totally inadequate and tempt you to give up. Remember, 'mistakes' can be sources of learning and reminders that we are, after all, human.

Gluttony

Taken literally, gluttony is eating or drinking to excess. Underlying this notion, however, is the idea that the glutton can't stop consuming when already fully nourished. In living beings there is a balanced flow of taking in and giving out. The glutton remains anchored within the modality of 'taking in' at a time when he should move the energy for action to 'giving out'. He is driven to consume what he has now, even if there is more than he needs, before anyone else can consume it. While we must consume to survive, gluttonous consumption destroys our physical, psychological and spiritual health and wellbeing.

We have broadened the concept of gluttony to encompass the full range of excesses in life that being a leader of people and organisations makes available to us. This includes a plethora of long lunches and the consumption of a range of 'executive perks' unavailable to others, such as massive bonuses, luxury cars and mansions. It also includes the over-consumption of precious resources by individuals, organisations and communities—fleets of gas-guzzling four-wheel drives that seldom escape the city streets; wasteful consumption of water and energy by industry; and use of agricultural methods that consume the fertility of the soil.

We live in a gluttonous society, where our bodies are overstuffed with food, our minds overstuffed with information and our lives overstuffed with material goods. Yet still we long for more.

What is the resolution?

A wise leader lives sparingly and touches the world's resources lightly. He takes only what is necessary for his personal wellbeing and knows how to share with others. He can give out as well as take in. Similarly, he ensures that the organisation he leads uses resources efficiently and with respect for the needs of the environment and society so that it contributes to their sustainability.

At both a personal and an organisational level, the wise leader creates a balance between what he and his organisation consume and what is given back to the world for others to share.

Greed

Of all the deadly sins, greed is the most common in organisational life. Recently we have been confronted with greed on a massive scale that has destroyed huge companies and is threatening stock market values as a whole. The newspapers have featured a parade of greedy senior executives who face court cases over the personal misappropriation of millions and the destruction of billions of dollars of shareholders' assets.

Greed elevates the desire for material wealth over spiritual development. The ancient Greek philosophers devoted considerable attention to greed. Aristotle saw wisdom as the virtue of knowing right from wrong and Antiphanes reputedly claimed: 'The quest for riches darkens the sense of right and wrong.'

Greed has become institutionalised at the core of our society. Monopolies are established on the basis of greed—the desire to have unlimited power to establish prices and control markets. The greed of dominating the market, creating obstacles or barriers to entry so no-one else can share in wealth was a major concern for Adam Smith, the father of capitalist economics. Today, however, there are managers and managerial theorists who have raised this to a virtue.

As a consequence of greed's power to divert corporate leaders from wisdom's path, regulatory bodies have been created solely to control greed in many areas of economic life. Nevertheless, there are still organisations that pollute the environment, sell dangerous and poor quality goods, ignore medical and scientific warnings about their products, exploit employees, destroy and deplete natural resources, hide business dealings that might compromise share prices and engage in illegal business transactions. Ultimately, these things are not done by organisations in abstract but by individuals and groups who live the maxim 'greed is good'.

What is the resolution?

The wise leader has a deep sense of responsibility to her society, to the environment and to the world as a delicate, intricately linked ecosystem. She understands that the true value of organisations and societies is that they create value for all citizens. The wise leader also keeps future generations in mind. She asks: 'What is the legacy I and my organisation will leave to those who come after me?'

Envy

Envy is the desire to possess that which others have but which we lack. At work, envy can exist in many forms. We may, for example, resent the promotion of a colleague or view every new, talented employee as a threat to our own job. We may envy our boss his position while avoiding responsibility in ours.

Envy and jealousy are closely related and have in common the desire to possess something or someone at any cost—to the point where these emotions result in destructive behaviours that shatter relationships. The envious person values things above people; the jealous person tries to control others rather than let them be free. Ironically, the result of envy and jealousy can be the loss of the very thing or relationship we value.

Envy and jealousy arise out of the fear of personal inadequacy. Our sense of inadequacy is so profound that we believe we cannot survive without the things and relationships that seem to give others power. We cry: 'If only I had what she has' or 'If only I could control his or her attention and love.' What we are lacking is actually something within ourselves, not an object or another person.

What is the resolution?

A wise leader is not driven by envy and does not jealously guard his relationships, knowledge, expertise and power. He shares knowledge and expertise and knows greatness is not achieved through acquiring worldly possessions or others' capabilities, or by owning others.

A wise leader is confident of his strengths and success and rejoices in others' strengths and successes, supporting others in going further. Similarly, he looks to develop the organisation's distinctive competencies and its unique contribution to the industry, and to form collaborative alliances that increase the combined capabilities of the emerging partnerships.

Lust

Traditionally, lust has been defined as extreme sexual desire that is so focused on the body of another that it ignores their spirit.

Clearly we have bodies and need to understand the biological nature of our being, including our sexuality. We are not simply free-floating minds or disembodied spirits. What the body needs for survival and reproduction is normally pleasurable and can be a source of great joy and ecstasy. To appreciate our biological nature is, however, different from being entrapped within it. Wisdom affirms both the body and spirituality.

Lust is a powerful force in human life and often forms a vital part of our hidden interpersonal underworld (and hence is the subject of gossip, jokes and often fear). In the workplace it can be expressed through the use of power to win sexual favours from those of lower status. Or people can use sex manipulatively to gain promotion or special treatment from those of higher status.

We widen the notion of lust beyond sexual gratification, however, to include what we call 'ego gratification'. Ego gratification is the use of others to serve our own ends, regardless of their wants or interests. When we use others in this way we deny their spirituality.

What is the resolution?

The wise leader is at ease with her sexuality and establishes relationships on a basis of respect and without manipulation. She is sensitive to the responses of others and to differences in status. She is aware of her own sexual desires and sexual energy and their potential to create havoc in the workplace, and she tempers them with care and consideration for others.

She is secure enough in her self-esteem to be able to forgo ego gratification if it involves ignoring or exploiting the needs and wants of others. She understands that identifying with others' needs, rather than exploiting them, enlarges the spirit. She uses her life energy to enhance the spiritual life of the organisation.

Vanity

When we think we are more important than anyone else and that nothing can function without us, it is time to remember Charles De Gaulle's statement that 'the graveyards are full of indispensable people'.

Vanity is the belief that our own abilities or attributes are superior to those of others, and that all others should revere us. The vain person lives in constant fear that he is not exceptional, or will lose his exceptional attributes or abilities. His self-worth is tied up in a constant attempt to prove his superiority to himself and to others.

Much of modern advertising appeals to our sense of vanity by encouraging us to try to appear younger, more beautiful, wealthier and more famous than others. It assures us that we can be forever young; that we can secure higher social status by buying an expensive car; that we can find true happiness and security in an insurance policy.

What is the resolution?

The wise leader values his abilities and attributes, but accepts that their value today may disappear tomorrow. He looks beyond youth or beauty because he knows these things are fleeting and have little to do with who a person really is or what a person can achieve.

Change is necessary and inevitable—something to be celebrated, not feared. The wise leader has faced his own inevitable death and knows he can be replaced. He works to ensure that there are others even more effective than himself to take his place so that he can go on to the next challenge on the road to wisdom.

Wrath

Wrath is a 'feeling of intense anger' that goes beyond mere anger to blind rage, fury and hate. It occurs around us in the forms of road rage, child and spouse beating, punch-ups, industrial sabotage and terrorist bombings.

Modern organisations generate pressures that create wrath. People in authority often try to control by fear because they live in fear. In the short term they may extort more output from their fearful employees, but in the long term their behaviour creates anger and destroys the basis of trust on which effective organisations depend. Nevertheless, many organisations reward such behaviour.

Wrath diminishes our ability to make rational decisions on the basis of evidence. Wrath acts like a black hole that sucks in all those around it. Wrath proceeds from judgment rather than acceptance and is a denial of compassion and love.

Of course anger, which is not as intense as wrath, can be a positive force. The angry person cares enough about something or someone to be emotionally involved. The real enemy of relationships is indifference. Anger can be a cleansing fire that confronts us with the raw reality of a relationship and replaces phoniness with honesty. The issue is how we handle anger. Can we use it to sweep away pretence and niceties so we can relate at a deeper level?

What is the resolution?

The truly wise leader knows how to channel the energy of anger to use it as a positive force. Her judgments are not made in haste, nor clouded by emotions like anger. She maintains relationships, even where this is difficult, and does not lose sight of others as human beings worthy of respect. She knows how to be calm and how to calm those around her through her presence.

She also ensures that the organisation does not engage in 'industrial road rage', causing widespread havoc in the industry through unsustainable cost-cutting, unethical cutthroat manoeuvres directed at wiping out competitors, or vindictive IR policies.

Sloth

Traditionally, sloth has meant apathy and inactivity in the practice of virtue. In other words, sloth is a lack of commitment to the active pursuit of virtue; not caring about right or wrong, rather than actually doing wrong.

Sloth is the ultimate sin because it represents the quenching of enthusiasm of the human spirit itself. It is the attitude of 'couldn't care less'. All the other sins relate to the passions and leaders often succumb to them because leaders are passionate people. But to be indifferent to values, to be indifferent to life, not to care, to be content to be carried along on the tide of life—this is the antithesis of leadership.

Leaders in the workplace often define slothfulness as absence of effort on the part of employees. They accuse employees who avoid effort of being 'shirkers'. They attempt to handle this by instituting more surveillance and closer supervision. This may include computer-based systems to monitor output, even on a moment-to-moment basis, as in many call centres. The organisation develops a managerial culture of constant surveillance, control, suspicion and punishment that destroys innovation and creativity and creates active revolt, subversion or passive resistance.

The perceptive leader asks the questions: 'Why are these people so de-motivated at work? What have I, my colleagues or our managerial predecessors done to deprive the people in this organisation of a sense of purpose and vision, to destroy the trust that is vital for living?'

What is the resolution?

A wise leader founds the organisation he leads on the basis of some worthy purpose and inspires those around him to contribute to that purpose. He knows how to motivate, reward and discipline without compromising the identity of those he leads. He understands the task at hand, but also how to manage the vital human relations inherent within each task.

He knows that organisational conditions, procedures, rules and regulations may destroy motivation, or that there may be a fundamental relationship problem in the workplace. He revels in overcoming such challenges by creating a living, meaningful vision that people are proud to commit to.

Conclusion

Wise leaders know how difficult it is to achieve realistic self-knowledge. So they seek relevant, specific and precise feedback. To such a person, there is no positive or negative feedback, only relevant feedback, which they take in, learn from and use to make appropriate changes to the way they operate. Wise leaders choose to defend principles and ideals, not their own egos.

While masters are a source of wisdom, ultimately we must each find our own wisdom and test it through experience, avoiding leaders who are authoritarian, power-oriented, egoistic and dogmatic. The value base underlying this search for wisdom can be found within the chapters of this book. The truly wise are compassionate and courageous; value integrity and humility; have a sense of humour void of sarcasm; and are passionate, but never to the point of distraction.

The wise leader has an undying willingness to listen and to learn, and a natural tendency to act as a mentor, never as dominator.

Most importantly, the wise are generous with their greatest wealth—their wisdom. They inspire us, not to do what they have done or what they say, but to seek the source of our own wisdom within ourselves. The greatness we need to lead others we can only find from within.

1 Integrate knowledge and experience and express them through action.

2 Choose a spiritual path and make it your own.

3 Hold to your path despite distraction.

4 Understand the stage you are at on the path to mastering wisdom.

5 Develop the skills appropriate to the stage of mastery you are at.

6 Use the ten guidelines outlined in this chapter as an aid to seeking wisdom.

7 Steer clear of the seven deadly sins of leadership and find your source of wisdom within yourself.

For further exploration

Dexter Dunphy's recommendations:

—D Chatterjee, *Leading Consciously: A Pilgrimage Towards Self Mastery*, Butterworth-Heinemann, New Delhi, 1999.

A deeply spiritual book by a leading Indian management professor. He draws upon the spiritual traditions of India to describe what he calls 'actionable spirituality' as the basis for managerial leadership.

—RE Quinn, *Change the World: How Ordinary People Can Accomplish Extraordinary Results*, Jossey-Bass, San Francisco, 2000.

A book that shows how each of us can go beyond the struggle for self-interested survival to lead by awakening the potential for creative change in all living systems. However, we can only reap the benefits of this if we are prepared to pay the costs.

—PB Baltes & UM Staudinger, 'A metaheuristic (pragmatic) to orchestrate mind and virtue toward excellence', *American Psychologist*, vol. 2, no. 1, 2000, pp. 122–36.

This article provides an excellent review of research and theorising on wisdom. More importantly, this special issue of the *American Psychologist* is an excellent introduction to the discipline of Positive Psychology.

Tyrone Pitsis's recommendations:

—S Fineman (ed.), *Emotion in Organizations*, Sage, London, 2000. This book covers a broad range of research and theory about emotion at the individual, group, social and organisational levels. Fantastic chapters by leading authors, with topics ranging from compassion in organisations to emotional intelligence and emotion in the police force. Much of what leaders do, and are, is emotional—this book is, therefore, a must read.

—J Ralston Saul, *The Unconscious Civilization*, House of Anasi Press, Canada, 1995. This book represents beautifully what this chapter is all about. Our society is dominated by corporatism and conformism at the expense of the 'individual' and of 'democracy'. Saul argues we must reflect upon, and rediscover, the meaning of 'individualism' and 'democracy' and then apply that knowledge in a way that allows us to become a 'conscious civilisation' once again.

Also recommended—anything by Robert E Quinn, Fred Luthans, Debashis Chatterjee or Martin EP Seligman.

Acknowledgments

Chapter 1 Humility

Mark Strom

Table 1.1: The traits of great leaders is based on material from Jim Collins, *Good to Great*, Harper Business, New York, 2001.

Chapter 3 Integrity

Margaret Thorsborne

Figure 3.1: The compass of shame was adapted from DL Nathanson, *Shame and Pride: Affect, Sex and the Birth of Self*, WW Norton, New York, 1992; and DL Nathanson, 'About emotion' in DL Nathanson (ed.), *Knowing Feeling*, WW Norton, New York, 1996.

Chapter 5 Humour

Colin Benjamin

The 'Norm' cartoons used in this chapter appear with the kind permission of: *Life. Be in it*.™, Alec Stitt and Recreation Australia—respectively, the copyright originator and minders of Norm.

Norm's Poem was first published in *The Australian Journal for Health, Physical Education and Recreation* (published by the Australian Council for Health, Physical Education and Recreation, South Australia) in June 1979.

Chapter 6 Passion

Charles Kovess

Earlier versions of some of the material in this chapter have appeared in Charles Kovess, *Passionate People Produce,* Nacson & Sons, Sydney, 1997; and Charles Kovess, *Passionate Performance*, Information Australia, Sydney, 2000.

DJ Wood's unpublished poem was written in 2001.

Chapter 7 Wisdom

Dexter Dunphy and Tyrone Pitsis

Table 7.1: Stages in achieving leadership mastery was adapted from HL Dreyfus, E Dreyfus & T Athenasion, *Mind over Machine: The Power of Human Intuition and Expertise in the Era of the Computer*, Free Press, New York, 1986; and RE Quinn, *Change the World: How Ordinary People Can Accomplish Extraordinary Results*, Jossey Bass, San Francisco, 2000.

Figure 7.1: Skills of effective leaders was adapted from D Dunphy, A Giffiths & S Benn, *Organizational Change for Corporate Sustainability*, Routledge, London, 2003, p. 276.

Bibliography

Chapter 1 Humility

Aristotle, *Nicomachean Ethics* (trans. T Irwin), Hackett Publishing Co., USA, 2000.

Aristotle, *Politics,* Book 3, Penguin, London, 1962.

Barrett, W, *Irrational Man: A Study in Existential Philosophy*, Mercury, London, July 1962.

Collins, J, *Good to Great*, Harper Business, New York, 2001.

Collins, J, 'Level 5 leaders: The triumph of humility and fierce resolve', *Harvard Business Review*, January 2001.

Confucius, *The Analects of Confucius* (trans. A Waley), Random House, USA, 1989.

Crawford, E, *Over My Tracks: A Remarkable Life*, Penguin, Melbourne, 1993.

Ebury, S, *Weary: The Life of Sir Edward Dunlop*, Penguin, Melbourne, 1995.

Lao Tzu, *Tao Te Ching*, Penguin, London, 1963.

McCain, Senator J, 'Occasional address at Valley Forge Military Academy and College', Philadelphia, Pennsylvania, 30 May 1999 at http://mccain.senate.gov/vfmaspch.htm.

Mackay, H, *Turning Point: Australians Choosing Their Future*, Macmillan, Sydney, 1999.

Plutarch, *Moralia*, volume VII (trans. PH De Lacy & B Einarson), Loeb Classical Library, USA, 1959.

Pullen, J, *Joshua Chamberlain: A Hero's Life and Legacy,* Stackpole, Mechanicsburg, 1999.

Ralston Saul, J, *On Equilibrium*, Penguin, London, 2001.

Sacks, Rabbi J, 'Humility: An endangered virtue', at www.jewish-holiday.com/humvirtue.html.

Shaara, M, *Killer Angels*, Ballantine Books, New York, 1974.

Strom, M, *Reframing Paul: Conversations in Grace and Community*, InterVarsity Press, Chicago, 2000.

Williamson, M, 'Our deepest fear', in M Williamson, *A Return To Love: Reflections on the Principles of a Course in Miracles*, Harper Collins, 1996.

Yåuzan Daidåoji, *The Code of the Samurai* (trans. AL Sadler), Charles E Tuttle Co., USA, 1988.

Chapter 2 Courage

Allen, RE (trans.), 'The Crito', in *The Dialogues of Plato*, vol. 1, Yale University Press, New Haven, 1984.

Bishop, S, 'The strategic power of saying no', *Harvard Business Review*, November 1999.

Byrne, JA & B Nussbaum, 'Inside McKinsey' and 'Can trust be rebuilt', *BusinessWeek*, 8 July 2002.

Collingwood, H & D Coutu, 'Jack on Jack: The HBR interview', *Harvard Business Review*, February 2002.

Collins, J, *Good to Great*, Harper Business, New York, 2001.

Cornwell, R, 'Stop the madness', interview with JK Galbraith, *The Globe and Mail Canada*, 6 July 2002.

Farkas, CM, 'Setting the direction: Lou Gerstner at American Express', *Harvard Business Review*, December 2001.

Goleman, D, 'What makes a leader', *Harvard Business Review*, November–December 1998.

Goleman, D, 'Leadership that gets results', *Harvard Business Review*, March 2000.

Goleman, D, R Boyatzis & A McKee, 'Primal leadership', *Harvard Business Review*, December 2001.

Haines, J, *Maxwell*, Macdonald, London, 1988.

Heifetz, R, 'The work of leadership', *Harvard Business Review*, December 2001.

Kellerman, B, 'Breakthrough leadership', *Harvard Business Review*, December 2001.

Kidder, R, 'Moral courage: A White Paper', *Institute for Global Ethics*, Maine, USA, 2001.

Kotter, J, 'Why transformation efforts fail', *Harvard Business Review*, March 1995.

Kotter, J, *Leading Change*, Harvard Business School Press, Boston, 1996.

Lord Moran, *The Anatomy of Courage*, Constable, London, 1945.

Newman, B, *The 10 Laws of Leadership Vision*, Bill Newman International, North Sydney, 1993.

Peace, W, 'The hard work of being a soft manager', *Harvard Business Review*, December 2001.

Tedlow, R, 'What titans can teach us', *Harvard Business Review*, December 2001.

Watson, D, *Recollections of a Bleeding Heart: A Portrait of Paul Keating PM*, Knopf, Australia, 2002.

Chapter 3 Integrity

Braithwaite, J, *Crime, Shame and Reintegration,* Cambridge University Press, Cambridge, 1989.

Center for Creative Leadership, *Tools for Developing Successful Executives,* Center for Creative Leadership, Greensboro, 1997.

Clemmer, J, 'Values-based leadership has huge pay-off', *Pathways to Performance: A Guide to Transforming Yourself, Your Team, and Your Organisation*, Prima Publishing, Rocklin CA, 1995.

Darwin, C, *The Expression of the Emotions in Man and Animals,* University of Chicago Press, Chicago, 1965 (originally published in 1872).

Demos, EV, *Exploring Affect: The Selected Writings of Silvan S Tomkins,* Cambridge University Press, Cambridge, 1995.

Goleman, D, R Boyatzis & A McKee, *The New Leaders: Transforming the Art of Leadership into the Science of Results*, Little, Brown, London, 2002.

Kelly Jr, VC, 'Affect and the redefinition of intimacy', in DL Nathanson (ed.), *Knowing Feeling,* WW Norton, New York, 1996.

Kouzes, JM & BZ Posner, *The Leadership Challenge: How to Get Extraordinary Things Done in Organizations*, Jossey-Bass, San Francisco, 1997.

Lombardo, MM & RW Eichinger, *Preventing Derailment: What To Do Before It's Too Late,* Center for Creative Leadership, Greensborough, 1989.

Maccoby, M, 'Do you know if you are trusted?', *Research Technology Management*, vol. 45, no.4, July–August 2002.

Manske, F, *Secrets of effective leadership: A practical guide to success,* Leadership Education & Development, USA, 1999.

Nathanson, DL, *Shame and Pride: Affect, Sex, and the Birth of Self,* WW Norton, New York, 1992.

Nathanson, DL, 'About emotion', in DL Nathanson (ed.), *Knowing Feeling,* WW Norton, New York, 1996.

Sarros, JC, JH Gray & I Densten, 'Key findings: Australian Business Leadership Survey', *Australian Business Leadership Survey*, AIM–Monash University, 2001.

Tomkins, SS, *Affect / Imagery / Consciousness*, vol. 1, *The Positive Affects*, Springer, New York, 1962.

Tomkins, SS, *Affect / Imagery / Consciousness*, vol. 2, *The Negative Affects*, Springer, New York, 1963.

Tomkins, SS, *Affect / Imagery / Consciousness*, vol. 3, *The Negative Affects—Anger and Fear*, Springer, New York, 1963.

Tomkins, SS, *Affect / Imagery / Consciousness*, vol. 4, *Cognition—Duplication and Transmission of Information*, Springer, New York, 1963.

Tomkins, SS, 'Script theory', in J Aronoff, AI Rabin & RA Zucker (eds), *The Emergence of Personality,* Springer, New York, 1987.

Chapter 4 Compassion

Commonwealth of Australia, *Karpin Report* (Report of the Industry Task Force on Leadership and Management Skills), AGPS, Canberra, 1995.

Eliot, TS, *Four Quartets*, Harvest Books, USA, 1974.

Marshall, P, quoting Pierre-Jean Fabre on alchemy, in *The Philosopher's Stone*, Pan Macmillan, UK, 2002.

Chapter 5 Humour

Adair, J, *Effective Leadership,* Gower, Aldershot, UK, 1983.

Allen, W, 'Humorous quotes attributed to Woody Allen', *Jest For Pun*, at
http://www.workinghumor.com/quotes/woody_allen.shtml.

Apps, JW, *Leadership for the Emerging Age,* Jossey-Bass, UK, 1994.

Bennis, W, *On Becoming a Leader,* Hutchinson Business Books, USA, 1989.

Cavett, D, quoted on the web page *Amusing Quotes*, at
http://www.amusingquotes.com/h/c/Dick_Cavett_1.htm.

Cleese, J, quoted in A Klein (ed), *Quotations to Cheer You Up When the World is Getting You Down*, Wings Books, New York, 1991.

Daly, J, quoting Al Capone, in 'History lessons', *Business 2.0*, June 2001.

Diller, P, quoted on the web site *The Cheers Project*, at
http://www.cheersproject.com/quotes.html.

Greenleaf, R, 'Unpublished manuscript', quoted in MS Peck & P Senge (eds), *Reflections on Leadership,* John Wiley & Sons, New York, 1995.

Hickman,C, *Mind of a Manager Soul of a Leader,* John Wiley & Sons, New York, 1990.

Marx, G, quoted in Paul McGee, *Health, Healing and the Amuse System: Humor as Survival Training,* Kendall/Hunt, 1999.

White, EB, 'The humor paradox', *New Yorker,* 27 September 1952.

Wooten, P, 'Humor: An antidote for stress', *Holistic Nursing Practice,* vol.10, no. 2, 1996, pp. 49–55.

Chapter 6 Passion

Bartholomeusz, S, 'The sick emperor of capitalism needs urgent fixing', *Age,* 29 June 2002.

Bernacki, E, *Wow! That's a Great Idea!,* Perspectives Publishing, Melbourne, 2001.

Buckminster Fuller, Dr R, *Critical Path,* St Martin's Press, New York, 1981.

Brouard, J, 'Quick! The price of having it now', *Australian Financial Review Magazine,* May 1998.

Gettler, L, 'Australian management mantras: Avoid conflict and duck for cover', *Age,* 6 December 2001.

de Geus, A, *The Living Company,* Harvard Business School Press, Boston, 2002.

Gibran, K, *The Prophet,* Heinemann, London, 1970.

Hamel, G, *Leading the Revolution,* Harvard Business School Press, Boston, 2000.

Kelleher, H, interview in *Fortune Magazine,* November 1998.

Kohler, A, 'System of governance shown to be bordering on the useless', *Australian Financial Review,* 29 June 2002.

Kovess, C, *Passionate People Produce,* Nacson & Sons, Sydney, 1997.

Kovess, C, *Passionate Performance,* Information Australia, Sydney, 2000.

Patanjali, quoted in W Dwyer, *Wisdom of the Ages, A Modern Master Brings Eternal Truth into Everyday Life,* HarperCollins, USA, 1998.

Pfeffer, J, *The Human Equation,* Harvard Business School Press, Boston, 1998.

Thomas, B, *Walt Disney,* Pocket Books, USA, 1998.

Chapter 7 Wisdom

Castaneda, C, *Separate Reality: Further Conversations with Don Juan*, Pocket Books, New York, 1973.

Chatterjee, D, *Leading Consciously: A Pilgrimage Towards Self Master*, Butterworth-Heinemann, New Delhi, 1999.

Davis, S & C Meyer, *Blur: The Speed of Change in the Connected Economy*, Perseus Publishing, New York, 1997.

Deikman, AJ, *The Observing Self: Mysticism and Psychotherapy*, Beacon Press, Boston, 1982.

Dreyfus, HL, E Dreyfus & T Athenasion, *Mind over Machine: The Power of Human Intuition and Expertise in the Era of the Computer*, Free Press, New York, 1986.

Dunphy, D, A Giffiths & S Benn, *Organizational Change for Corporate Sustainability*, Routledge, London, 2003.

Hamel, G & C H Prahalad, *Competing for the Future*, Harvard Business School Press, Boston, 1994.

Quinn, RE, *Change the World: How Ordinary People Can Accomplish Extraordinary Results*, Jossey-Bass, San Francisco, 2000.

Storr, A, *Feet of Clay—A Study of Gurus*, Harper Collins, London, 1996.

Zohar D & I Marshall, *SQ—Connecting with our Spiritual Intelligence*, Bloomsbury, New York and London, 2000.

Index

Page numbers in **bold** print refer to main entries

Powell, John, 185
pressure, 43–4
pride, false, 74
problem solving, 64, 80, 97, 182–3
product tampering, 46
productivity, 146–7
products, valuing, 92
proficiency, 174, 176
profit, 105, 149
profitability, 146–7
The Prophet, 143

real estate agencies, 62
reality, acceptance of, 165, 180–1
reason, 20, 174, 176
    passion &, 143–4
Recollections of a Bleeding Heart, 35
reductionism, **88–90**, 94
relationships, 68–9, 82, 128–9, 184–5
resolve, 42–3, 47
respect, 50, 148
responsibility, 142, 153–4, 165
restorative justice, 64, 67–8, 80
risk-taking, 155
rules, 173–5

Sacks, Jonathan, 10, 12, 13, 29
sales industry, 62
sarcasm, 115
satire, 115, 125
Saul, John Ralston, 19–20
secrecy, 74
Secrets of Effective Leadership, 76–7
self-awareness, 135, 156, 160, 180
    lack of, 37
    leadership &, **36–7**, 47, 54–5, 165
self-belief, 42–3, 54
self-control, 5, 6, 27
self-interest, 20
self-knowledge, 160, 165, 179, 195
self-perception, 15–16
self-reflection, 75, 106–8, 171
Seneca, 4, 6, 27
serotonin, 117–18
service, valuing, 92

shame, **67–71**
    case studies, 73–4, 76
    in workplace, 71–5
shareholders, 149, 152
Sherman, William T., 33
short-term thinking, 41, 105, 144–6
simple-easy dichotomy, 139–40
sloth, 188, 194–4
Smith, Darwin E., 42–3
Smith, Frederick, 43
Socrates, 34
'soft management', 44
spiritual dimension of leadership, 139
spiritual intelligence, 181
spirituality, 139, 160–1, 165, 172,
    186–7, 196
sporting competitors, 144
staff turnover, 148
stereotypes, 180
Storr, Anthony, 177
strategies, 175
stress, 148
success, 153, 186–7
synergy, 157–9, 163

tall poppy syndrome, 24–5, 27
team spirit, 139
teamwork, 47, 157, 165
technology, 184
Tedlow, Richard S., 45–6
Telstra Corporation, 150
The 10 Laws of Leadership Vision,
    51–2
Thomas, Bob, 152
time, misuse of, 74
Tomkins, Silvan S., 69–71, 75, 78
Tools for Developing Successful
    Executives, 79
Travel Related Services (TRS), 48
trust, 40, 47, 50
    lack of, 62–3
    loss of, 40, 62–4, 71
truth, 41, 142
Turning Point, 25
Twain, Mark, 34

MANAGEMENT TODAY

The Australian Institute of Management's national monthly magazine
Management Today keeps you in touch with all the issues that matter –
leadership, globalisation, strategic thinking, e-management and much more.
It is Australia's only magazine focusing on the profession of management
and is a 'must read' for managers at all levels.

A free subscription to *Management Today* is one of the many bonuses
of AIM corporate and personal membership. However, additional or new
subscriptions are available for $55.00 (GST included) per year (ten issues
including postage and handling).

Please return by
post ...
fax (07) 3832 2497 ...
phone (07) 3227 4888 ...

or visit our website www.aim.com.au
and follow the links to *Management Today*.